# Shrubs and Decorative Evergreens

# Shrubs and Decorative Evergreens

Edited by Francis Stark & Conrad Link

**THE BOBBS-MERRILL COMPANY, INC.**
Indianapolis • New York

American edition reviewed
and adapted to U.S. conditions
by Conrad B. Link and Francis
C. Stark; Professors of
Horticulture; University of
Maryland; College Park.

# Contents

# Preface

Even in a garden of a quarter of an acre or so it is possible to grow quite comfortably 30 shrubs or so and a great deal more if one goes in for ground-cover and miniature shrubs. Yet the sheer number of shrubs from which one has to select is so bewilderingly large that anyone who becomes enchanted by shrubs, as one so easily can, is likely to plant far more than he really has room for.

Indeed, it is quite easy to put a whole garden down to shrubs and nothing else, for they are an enchanting group of plants. Yet perhaps in the long run, if one wants a wholly satisfying garden, one should make the shrubs the main feature and yet have little bays between them of one's favorite bulbs, herbaceous plants and even bedding plants. In the end it will create a more satisfyingly rich tapestry in the garden.

On the other hand if one has other interests to pursue at weekends, and most of us have — even the keenest of gardeners often have — and if one at the same time wants a garden that will give the greatest pleasure throughout the whole year for the least effort, then a garden devoted wholly or mainly to shrubs is the easiest way of attaining that ideal.

The main purpose of this little book is to make the choosing of shrubs easier, especially for the inexperienced gardener. And it has another purpose too. What this book will tell you, is the disadvantages of many shrubs — and that's worth knowing too.

The firethorn *Pyracantha* is typical of a shrub good at more than one season: it is effective both in flowers and fruit. This plant trained on a wall.

# 1 In Praise of Shrubs

A shrub is usually defined as a woody perennial that branches from or just above ground level. It differs from a herbaceous perennial in that it does not die down to ground level each winter but builds up a permanent framework of branches with every passing season. So, of course, does a tree, which is also a woody perennial, but a tree differs from a shrub in that it is usually defined as having a clean, unbranched stem for at least six feet above the ground.

Such a succinct definition does not, however, give the slightest idea of the sheer range of plants embraced by that definition. There are many hundreds of woody perennials that can be grown out of doors in some part of the United States. Of those some are highly ornamental and, in the main, easily grown shrubs which can readily be obtained from most garden centers and nurseries. Yet even this limited number of shrubs provides a variety of shape of growth, of flower color, form and season, of leaf shape, color and color changes that no other group of plants can match or even rival. Furthermore, once properly planted in soil that has been well prepared to suit their needs, they will become a permanent asset to the garden, needing little attention once established and increasing in size and beauty with each passing year.

To many people's minds the greatest virtue of shrubs is that they are inexpensive to buy when young, and that in terms of the ground they cover and the contribution they make to the garden as a whole, they are the finest investment in the plant kingdom. There is no other group of plants that will give such a rewarding return on capital laid out, nor is there any other group that will do so over so many years, or with so little effort.

To many other people's ways of thinking their greatest virtue is that any of them will completely smother the weeds that grow under them, and again, this is completely true: a great many will do just that, especially the evergreens. If that is what one wants care must be taken in the selection of shrubs, for not all of them will.

Yet to anyone who is looking at the garden with a view to creating a three-dimensional picture of lasting but eternally changing beauty, then it is the sheer diversity of shrubs that is their greatest virtue.

To many inexperienced gardeners a shrub is just a bushy thing with leaves and flowers. There is infinitely more to shrubs than just this. There are tiny little creeping shrubs that crawl along the ground, growing no more than a couple of inches high, and there are shrubs which, though slow-growing, ultimately reach the dimensions of a small tree. There are shrubs that grow upright, like a guardsman on parade, and others that spread themselves leisurely over the ground, leaning on it here and there and rooting as they go. There are many that form what can scarcely be better described than as shrubby shrubs, while there are others that weep, and still others that form mushroom-shaped bushes, while still others form pyramidal bushes. There are some that stand with their arms outstretched like scarecrows: some are as graceful in their way of growing as a ballerina, while others are rugged and gnarled as the olives on the Riviera. There are some that form wood hard enough to blunt even the sharpest pruning knife, others like the tree peonies *Paeonia suffruticosa* or the Californian tree poppy *Romneya coulteri* that are only semi-shrubby, about half of each year's growth dying back to the half that has ripened.

Probably the first thing the inexperienced gardener wants to know about a shrub is whether it has huge flowers. There certainly are many that do. Probably the largest flowers to be found on any shrub are those borne by the tree peonies *Paeonia suffruticosa* which can measure as much as eighteen inches across and come in every shade from purest white to scarlets and crimsons, with every conceivable shade of pink in between. The flowers can further vary in that they may be single, semi-double or very double. The fact that they are huge may not necessarily make them good garden plants: in many cases the flowers of the tree peonies are so huge and so heavy that they simply hang down and do not show properly; unless one props them up with stakes. The slightly smaller flowered forms are usually better garden plants. But there are other plants that have very large flowers, notably the magnolias, especially *Magnolia liliflora* 'Nigra', which has huge chalice-shaped flowers, or the paler pinkish-purple *Magnolia* × *soulaneana,* which flowers in spring on bare branches before the leaves open. The tree poppies *Romneya coulteri* and *Romneya* × *hybrida* also have huge flowers, six inches or more across.

The size of the individual flowers is not by any means the only criterion by which to judge the merit of a shrub. Lilacs, for example, have individually small flowers, but these are borne in huge numbers in densely packed spikes, and the spike as a whole may be just as effective or perhaps even more effective than an individual flower of the same size. In the spireas the flowers are relatively small, but again, produced in dense clusters creating by this grouping a far more effective inflorescence than the size of the individual flower would lead one to expect. Other shrubs, like *Cotinus coggygria* or the tamarisks present their flowers in very loose forms, often of a very open and airy nature, and yet borne in such abundance as to be effective, yet in a different manner.

The leaves of shrubs can vary too, and in many ways. They can be elliptic, palmate, pinnate, bipinnate, lanceolate, oval, oblong, obovate, cordate, trifoliate, ovate, hastate, lobed, linear and many other shapes. But that is only a beginning. They can be any of these shapes, but large or small. And, though most people tend to think of shrubs as having green leaves, they can be many other colors as well. Even in green there is enormous variation: the leaves of laurel and some rhododendrons and camellias are of a very dark black-green; while the leaves of *Pittosporum tenuifolium* are of a light silvery green and those of some of the magnolias a bright, fresh green. Other shrubs have leaves that are bronze, purple, copper, while still others have variegated leaves, margined, blotched or splashed with cream, yellow, white or pink.

The great majority of shrubs, if they flower, also produce seed heads, and a similar range of variation may be found among these. The great majority have rather dull seed heads, like those of lilacs or escallonias, yet many are more spectacular. The shrubby members of the clematis family have delightful feathery seedheads that shine with silver in the autumn light, while the smoke bush, *Cotinus coggygria* retains its delicate plumes long after they have finished flowering, imperceptibly changing from flowers to seedheads yet remaining beautiful all the time. Other shrubs like many of the cotoneasters are grown for their colorful berries: these are usually red or orange but there are shrubs like *Callicarpa bodinieri giraldii* (syn. *giraldiana*) in which the berries are an unexpected bright violet and *Symplocus paniculata* in which the berries are a singularly brilliant turquoise.

The bark of shrubs can vary just as much, and there are a number of willows and dogwoods grown solely for the brilliant coloring, usually bright red or bright yellow, of their young twigs in winter. They need to be pruned hard each spring for these bark effects to be seen at their best.

Then there is the variability of the flowering season of shrubs. The season starts with the witch hazels, notably *Hamamelis mollis* which is in flower in very early January in a mild winter, its spidery yellow blossoms

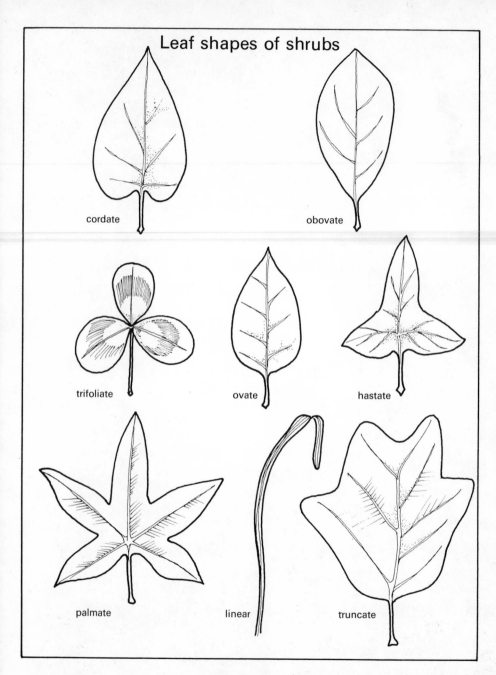

# Leaf shapes of shrubs

cordate

obovate

trifoliate

ovate

hastate

palmate

linear

truncate

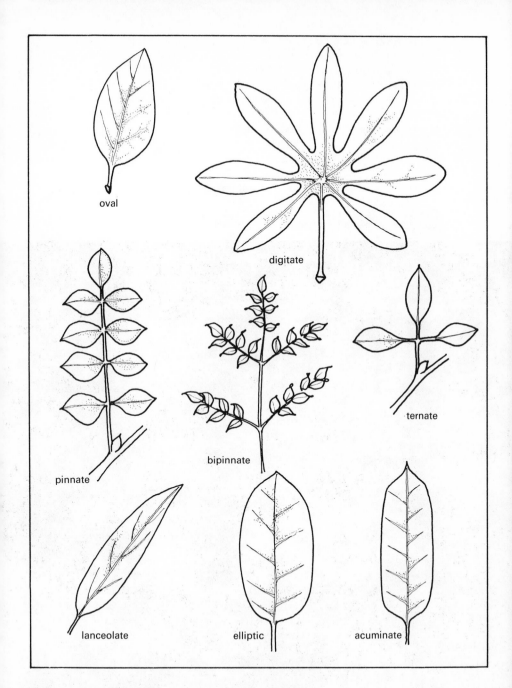

oval

digitate

pinnate

bipinnate

ternate

lanceolate

elliptic

acuminate

13

giving the air around the shrub a rich scent. This is followed by the wintersweet, *Chimonanthus praecox,* and a little later, by *Cornus mas* in February and into March. As the season goes on the number of shrubs in flower increases until June, a month which probably has more shrubs in flower than any other month of the year. After that the number in flower diminishes again. By some strange chance, many of the shrubs which flower after mid-summer have white flowers. The last shrub of all to

The Venetian smoke bush *Cotinus coggyria* retains its delicate, smoke-like flower plumes long after the actual flowering is past.

The sheer diversity of shrubs makes choosing the right ones for a small garden difficult. Most people think of rhododendrons as flowering plants. The one shown here, *Rhododendron beauravoides,* is grown chiefly for the rusty felt on the back of its large leaves.

flower is probably the Killarney strawberry tree *Arbutus unedo,* which produces its white, scented lily-of-the-valley, type flowers in November, together with the rich orange-red lichi-like fruits which have taken a whole year to ripen.

From the gardener's point of view the ideal shrub would be one which had an attractive habit of growth, attractive green or variegated foliage, good flowers followed by attractive autumn coloring and then by brightly colored fruits with, for good measure, good bark color in the dead of winter. Fortunately there is no shrub which quite measures up to this impossible ideal. Because of this, in order to achieve all these effects, one has to select a number of different shrubs, each one of which contributes one or more of these qualities to the group planting, and that is where skill is required in selecting and planting a shrub garden.

# 2 Making the Most of Shrubs

Such is the diversity of shrubs that a garden can be planted with them and with virtually nothing else and still be a joy through every week of the year — though perhaps the garden might achieve a slightly richer texture if some limited use were made of herbaceous ground-cover plants and both spring and autumn flowering bulbs, some of which could perhaps be planted in the lawn to add another dimension to the garden, and this is possible in even quite a small garden, one of a quarter of an acre or less.

The term 'shrubbery' is a rather outmoded one now, and carries with it connotations of rather gloomy Victorian plantings of deadly dull evergreens, especially privets, which are still seen in many public parks and places. Yet perhaps it is precisely because of these extremely dull plantings that pure shrubberies passed out of fashion, and the so-called 'mixed border' (i.e. a border containing a mixture of both herbaceous and shrubby material) came to replace it. In all fairness to the Victorians, it should be stressed that they simply did not have the range of colorful flowering and foliage shrubs available to them that are so easily accessible to every gardener today. It is a simple matter of history. The great majority of the most exciting shrubs that can be grown in gardens today have been collected since Victorian times. Indeed, if one takes the Victorian shrubbery as one's example of what can be achieved in the way of a pure shrub garden, one is likely to go away in disgust and put the whole garden down to concrete.

The simple fact is that nowadays there is such a wealth of shrubs, and that so many of them are really first rate, that anyone contemplating making an all-shrub garden is likely to finish up planting more than there is room for. This *embarras de richesses* means that one has to exercise some self-control in choosing one's plants, and discipline one's imagination, especially while reading nurserymen's descriptions of everything in their list. It is worth remembering that catalogues are produced to sell plants: each description of a plant is a mini-advertisement: and all it says of the plant in question may be true. Catalogues however seldom tell you what may be wrong with a particular plant, that it may die if you disturb its roots, that it will loose all its leaves if the local canine community adopts it by way of a lamp-post; nor do they tell you some of the other things that might affect your choice: such as many people come out in a rash from touching certain plants and that others develop hayfever from proximity to some plants.

Shrubs are probably the most economic way of planting a garden. The great majority can be bought for little more than the cost of a box of bedding plants and once planted need little further care. They will increase in size and stature year by year, and if well spaced apart, will join ranks and keep out weeds. Some, it is true, do better if pruned regularly, but for the lazy gardener there are so many to choose from that never need pruning that even this chore can be omitted. Some shrubs are better at keeping weeds down than others, and the chore of weeding can be minimized if only those shrubs which are really good ground-cover plants are selected. Yet even limitations like these embrace a sufficiently wide range of shrubs to make a really exciting garden.

The diversity of shrubs is so great that the real problem is not choosing what to include in one's garden but what to leave out. One can, in mild climates, have shrubs in flower every month of the year: in which case, in a small garden, one may well find that one has no more than one or two shrubs in flower at any one time of the year. Or one may choose to have a great burst of color in spring and early summer, but have the garden rather less colorful later in the year — though if this is the option one goes for, then it is worth remembering that roses are shrubs, and they will give color from mid-summer till first frosts, and that, if one leaves some beds for bedding plants, these will be at their best once the shrubs stop blooming.

There is another way of looking at the problem of what to plant, and that is to discount the flowers to begin with, and try to create something with the colors of the foliage of the shrubs, making the most of shrubs with colored or variegated leaves. At the same time changes in the texture of the plants are worth aiming for. And these are both effects that can easily be achieved with plants that can readily be obtained from most garden centers and nurseries. It is simply untrue that one needs obscure plants to achieve dramatic effect. Only when one has ensured that there will be the color and contrast of foliage in the garden, by the use of both deciduous and evergreen shrubs, should one start thinking in terms of flowers, though these are probably what most people will still consider first when they consider shrubs at all. The point about flowers is that they are usually over in a month or six weeks, whereas with deciduous shrubs the foliage is colorful for about seven to eight months of the year, and with evergreens for the full twelve months.

However, gardening is an art and what matters most, especially in a shrub garden, is not the individual plants that one chooses, but the total effect one creates by the way in which one combines the plants chosen. It is all very well and very easy to go through the catalogues and, having decided that one has room for fifteen shrubs, simply choose the fifteen mentioned in the catalogues that are all described as having large flowers. One will have a garden in which one has fifteen shrubs with large flowers: one will not have a pleasing garden. To achieve that one has to select plants, for example, with small flowers to contrast with the shrubs with large flowers; one needs plants with small leaves to contrast with plants with large leaves; one needs plants with grey leaves to contrast with the monotony of green — though there are as many shades of green as there are of pink. And one needs, in addition, to make use of plants with purple foliage as well as variegated foliage, and of plants with spiky leaves to contrast with those that have round leaves, of plants that have ferny foliage to contrast with those that have large, simple leaves. One needs to do all this if one is to make a shrub garden that will make a really pleasing visual impact. And all this is consistent with a garden that is economic to create and easy to maintain once planted.

There are other aspects which should also be considered. Among these are the habit of the shrub: thus rather than growing only bushy shrubs, it is worth including one or two that are of narrowly columnar habit, and carry their branches erect: it is also worth contrasting these with shrubs of a weeping habit, the majority of these forming mushroom-shaped bushes. There are a large number of shrubs which are more or less prostrate and most of these also happen to make excellent ground cover; these should be used with great freedom in any extended planting to grow not only at the front of the border but also to allow to run under those shrubs which do not keep weeds down.

In painting the visual picture of one's shrub garden some care and thought should be given to the mixture of evergreens and deciduous plants. Though evergreens are generally (but not invariably) better at keeping down weeds than deciduous shrubs and it is tempting to plant them in large quantities for that reason, evergreens, unrelieved by the inclusion of some deciduous shrubs, rapidly become monotonous unless care has been taken to include quite a high proportion of evergreens with variegated foliage, as well as plenty of contrast in foliage size and shape. Even then, the fact that the evergreens are always there, always the same, just increasing in size year by year and putting up their often very fine display of flowers, tends to make them boring. The inclusion of deciduous shrubs adds a different dimension to the border: it immediately makes the changing of the seasons noticeable. The bare twigs may not necessarily be attractive in winter, but they pave the way for the eternal surprise of spring, with its fresh green foliage — something which passes almost unnoticed when the evergreens put on their new leaves. And then there is autumn color, something which is rare among evergreens, though there are a number of evergreens, including conifers, whose leaves change color in winter. Evergreens also make the finest background of all for autumn color.

When it comes to using plants with variegated or colored leaves, again, some care should be given to locating these plants. A variegated deciduous shrub can be planted anywhere: it will come into its own in its own season. But a variegated evergreen will be far more appreciated if it is planted where it passes almost unnoticed throughout the summer, only to come into its own in winter when its presence is suddenly revealed by the falling of the leaves of some deciduous shrub that was planted in front of it. It is surprises of this sort that help to keep the garden interesting throughout the year.

The diversity of shrubs is their greatest asset: it is also their most bewildering facet, presenting such endless variety that making a decision between one plant and another can become a difficult matter. When one considers that a shrub is composed of only a limited number of elements — of flowers, leaves, fruits and stems, it really is surprising just how much variation can be found on such a simple theme. Yet to get the most out of a shrub garden, it is this diversity that one needs to exploit.

# 3 Choosing and Buying Shrubs

To the inexperienced gardener it must seem that there are so many shrubs that he could grow that it is almost impossible to choose which ones to grow. The question of what to plant is always a difficult one. Though there is a huge number of shrubs that can be grown out of doors in the United States, only a small number of them would ever really grow well in your garden — and this applies to everyone, no matter where his garden may be or how experienced a gardener he may be.

In every garden there are factors that limit the shrubs you can grow, and if one goes through these factors one can immediately eliminate an enormous number of shrubs.

**What will grow in your soil?**
The first thing to find out about any garden is what will grow in your garden. Earth may just be earth to most of us, but plants are slightly more fussy. Your soil may be clay or sandy, it may be peaty or it may be a good rich crumbly loam, and what will grow well on a dry, sandy soil will often simply rot away on a heavy clay soil. These terms describe what is known as the texture of the soil, and the texture of a soil can be changed in a number of ways, nearly always by adding more humus to it, though clay soils need coarse sand or clinkers added to increase drainage.

More important than the texture of your soil is whether it is acid, alkaline or neutral. This really is an important factor: if it is acid or neutral you will be able to grow all the shrubs that will endure in your climate, but if it is alkaline you will not be able to grow any rhododendrons, azaleas or camellias and quite a number of other exciting plants as well. You can plant them, but in the end they will succumb. On the other hand, this still leaves you with an enormous variety of first-rate shrubs to choose from: the important thing is to recognize what you cannot grow.

As to how to know whether your soil is acid or alkaline, the simplest way is to look around you. If there are rhododendrons in most of your

*Roses are all too often thought of as plants in a world apart. In fact, they are merely rather colorful flowering shrubs, and may be effective used just like other shrubs in the garden.*

neighbors' gardens, and if they look in good health, then the chances are that you are on an acid soil. If on the other hand there is not a rhododendron, azalea, or camellia to be seen for miles around, then you are almost certainly living in an alkaline area. Your weeds, too, can tell you quite a lot about your soil. If brake, for example, is common in your area, that is further indication that you are on acid soil.

A mose accurate way of determining the acidity or alkalinity of your soil is to use a soil-testing kit. There are a number of these on the market. Most of them are inexpensive to buy and easy to use. They can be bought from most garden centers or shops. You just follow the simple instructions that come with the kit, and in a very short time have an accurate knowledge of the soil in your garden. Acidity or alkalinity are measured on what is known as the pH scale. A reading of pH 7 means you have a neutral soil: a higher figure means it is alkaline, a lower figure that it is acid. When testing your soil it is worth taking readings from several different parts of the garden: it is quite likely that the builders will have scattered rubble in some part of the garden, and the soil there is likely to give a different reading from soil from a different part of the garden. In many states it is possible to have your soil tested by your local County Extension Agent.

If you are lucky enough to have a slightly acid or neutral soil, never add lime. One is often recommended to put old builder's rubble around clematis, since these plants are reputed to like lime in the soil. In fact nearly all the clematis will thrive without the lime, but if you want to grow a camellia next to the clematis, you've made yourself a problem, because it will not succeed.

### What will grow in your climate?
Climate is the next major factor involved in eliminating what will not grow in your garden. The higher the elevation or the further north you go, the colder the climate: the winters become longer and harder. In some areas the intensity of the sunlight in the summer decreases. This means that the further north you live the hardier the shrubs you need to grow. The eastern half of the U.S. generally enjoys greater rainfall than the western half and the rainfall is somewhat better distributed throughout the year. The East is well adapted to a wide variety of plant species, both deciduous and evergreen, with the tender species being delightfully grown in the South. The western states are subject to protracted periods of drought, with rainy seasons at times during the year, and species adapted are those that can tolerate these long drought periods. The Pacific North-

west, however, is excellent for the conifers, because of the frequent rains and high humidity. The North Central area is the coldest, bleakest part of the country, where anything that is not bone hardy has little chance of survival. Coastal areas are a special case, and plants on the seashore must be those that will tolerate some salt spray and heavy winds.

In the Southwest, wind is the greatest enemy of all. Unless you have some sort of shelter from winds, many shrubs will never become established at all. If you are lucky enough to have a garden that is already sheltered by other gardens and established plants, you will be able to grow a far wider range of shrubs than you will if your garden is on a bleak new site. If that is the case you will have to provide some sort of wind shelter in the way of fencing. A rigid fence provides little protection: it simply causes turbulence. The ideal fence is a permeable one that lets about 50 per cent of the wind through. This actually breaks the force of the wind.

The other great limiting factor is frost, especially late spring frosts, which kill off young growth: if they do this year after year, a shrub may never get any larger, may never flower and may in time die. Such late spring frosts hit hardest in frost-pockets, in valleys and in sheltered hollows. Just as hot air rises, so cold air pours downhill like water, always seeking the lowest point. If your garden is on a slope, make sure that there is a gap at the lowest part of the garden through which frosty air can drain away.

Many of the most beautiful shrubs are tender. The uninitiated may view the loss of such a shrub due to severe frost with great dismay, but the keener gardener will generally prefer to try it, and be grateful if it survives a run of a few mild winters and then succumbs: such gardeners will feel that it is better to have enjoyed a treasure for a few years, than never to have grown it at all. Those who are not prepared to take such risks should plant only those shrubs that are completely hardy.

**Finding out about Shrubs**
Most people when they want to find out what shrubs they could grow in their gardens turn to catalogues. They give glowing descriptions of every shrub they list, but in spite of that usually fail to give the reader any clear idea of what that shrub actually looks like in the flesh. Indeed, the best way to use catalogues is probably to regard them simply as check-lists of what you can buy from whom. Look through them, note what you think might be good in your garden but then try and see it growing somewhere before you buy it.

The importance of seeing shrubs before you buy them cannot be stressed strongly enough. Nor can the importance of selecting not individual shrubs but groups of shrubs, as combinations that will be more effective in the garden than single plants. There are many places where you can go to see shrubs growing well. Many public gardens, botanic gardens and arboretums have vast collections of shrubs, all clearly labelled, and usually grown well. To see them at their best, it is probably better to go to those private gardens that are open to the public, either all the year round or at selected weekends throughout the year. You can find details of these in your local newspaper. Many nurseries also have their own permanent collections of shrubs.

It is only when you see shrubs growing that you get any real idea of how they will look in your garden. And it is always worth carrying a note-pad and pencil to make a note of anything you find really striking. A word of warning, however: cross check with reference books to make sure that what you found interesting in that shrub is typical of it. It sometimes happens, though not too often, that one discovers later that that was the only time in ten years that that shrub had flowered really well.

It is always interesting to visit garden shows, but the show bench can be singularly misleading. What one sees is a spray of bloom. This gives one no idea of how the shrub grows, or how profusely it flowers. It doesn't even give one an idea of when the shrub flowers, for it may have been forced into flower early for the show, or retarded by keeping it cool. And if you see an excellent display of berries — bear in mind that they have probably been protected from birds by netting for several weeks, and that in your garden the birds might strip the lot in a week. Anyone visiting a show bench needs to adopt a decidely sceptical frame of mind!

**Where to Buy**
The ideal way to buy shrubs is to go to a good nursery and handpick the plants you want. This is not always possible, and all too often one has to buy by mail, thus trusting the nurseryman to select a good plant for you. Roughly speaking, if you buy by mail, then the earlier you send your order in the better the specimen you might receive. Ideally your order should be with the nurseryman by May or June for plants that are to be delivered in the autumn.

It is very tempting to buy shrubs from general stores, and often you will get good value for your money. However, unless you buy the shrubs the moment they arrive at the shop, you are likely to find them dried out with the heat of the store, the roots improperly wrapped, seldom damped, and are likely to arrive home with with a plant that is virtually — or sometimes completely — dead before you plant it. It is not always easy to tell whether a deciduous shrub is alive simply by looking at it. If in doubt scrape a little bark off a twig with your thumb-nail: if the layer under the bark is green and moist, the shrub is still fit. If it is white and dry, the shrub is already dead.

On the other hand, most people do not feel like planting their shrubs in

the autumn, which is the best time for most deciduous shrubs. It is when the grey winter passes, when the days start to get long, when the rains stop and the sun comes out in the spring, that one feels like planting one's garden. It's too late then to send an order to the nurseryman. If you want to buy shrubs at that time of the year, go to your local garden center. There you will find plants that have been specially grown in containers so that they can be planted at any time of year. These garden centers are a real boon to most gardeners, especially as they are usually open on weekends. However, there are quite a number of shrubs which do not do well in containers, and if you want to create a very individual garden, you will still have to go to a conventional nursery to obtain these. The only real disadvantage of garden centers is that, like most conventional retail outlets, they only stock those lines which they know they can sell well in their area, and if you go to the same garden center as all your neighbors you are likely to end up with much the same plants they have.

Shrubs and trees together
combine to give a mellow
texture to a garden.

# 4 Planting Shrubs

The whole secret of success with shrubs is to plant them properly, and that means in deeply dug soil whose texture has been suitably improved to meet the needs of the shrub that is about to be planted. Basically, there are very few shrubs that will grow in water-logged or poorly drained soil, and if you have that type of soil you will have to work harder to obtain success with shrubs (or any other plants for that matter), than you would with well-drained soil. You will need to lay drainage pipes in any area where you are going to grow groups of shrubs. The simplest to lay are unglazed drainage tiles, and these should be placed in the soil between 18 in. and 2 ft. deep, with a slight drop. The water they collect should empty into a soakaway which needs to be at least 4 ft. deep to be effective, and should be filled with large gravel. Once you've done that, prepare the soil for the shrubs as you would if you were planting in normal soil.

**Preparing the Shrub Border**
If one is planting a large area to shrubs it is far better to prepare the whole area than to dig individual holes for the individual shrubs. The shrubs will do better, and you will have the chance of growing ground-cover plants between the shrubs if you prepare the whole area properly in the first place. To prepare the ground you need to dig it deeply and thoroughly, and though this may seem hard work at the time, once it is done and the shrubbery has been planted, you will not have to do it again. And you can be certain that, all other things being right, the shrubs once planted will get away to a good start. If you don't prepare the ground properly the shrubs may take years to become established. The normal sequence of events is that the shrubs put on a little top growth and a lot of root growth their first year: their second year they grow vigorously and their third year they settle down to flowering, and will go on flowering with increasing splendor in each succeeding year.

The area to be occupied by the border should be marked out with stakes, and in general it is better to have a curving edge to the border than a straight line. Provided the curve is not too abrupt this will not make it any more difficult to mow, and the general effect will be far more pleasing. The soil should be double dug: that is you take out a trench about 15 in. wide and one spit (the depth of a spade) deep at one end and then carry the soil you have removed from that spit to the other end of the border. You then dig a similar spit beside that one, again taking the soil to the other end of the border. You then dig a second spit below where you dug the first spit, and again take the soil to the other end of the border. You have then established the starting sequence. You now take the second spit from the second trench you dug and turn it over into the bottom of the first trench you dug, and then start a third trench, turning the topsoil from that trench on to the top of the soil you have just turned over into your first trench, thus bringing it back to its original level. You continue this process, working your way back along the border until you come to the far end, where you fill the trenches with the soil you took out of the first trenches. To give the shrubs the best possible start in life it is worth mixing some well-rotted manure or compost into the soil in the lower spit as you turn it over: this encourages root development, and the extra fertilizing helps the shrubs get established.

With certain shrubs, especially rhododendrons, camellias and azaleas it is unnecessary to dig the manure in: these are surface-feeding plants. Instead, what you do is to mix peat or leaf-mold into the top spit, and then

Double digging, essential if one is preparing a large shrub border, and much to be preferred to digging individual holes for each of the shrubs in the border. The operation is described in detail in the text.

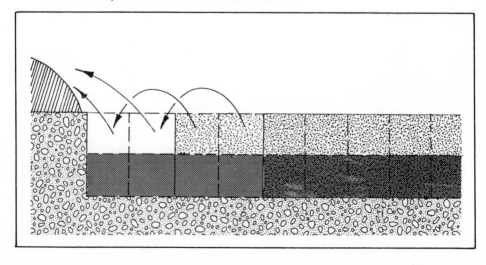

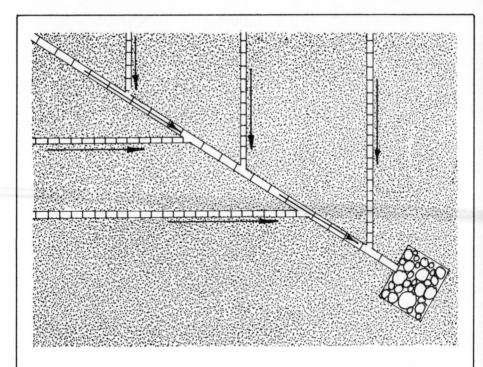

Drainage, showing how clay drainage tiles should be laid in herring-bone fashion, leading into a soakaway; the arrows indicate the direction in which the water flows. The drawing below shows how water enters the pipes and flows away.

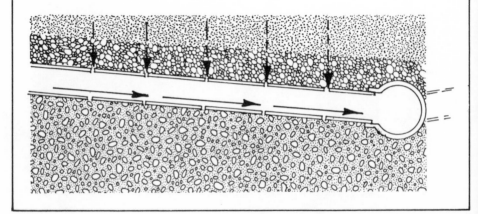

give the plants a good thick mulch of peat or leaf-mold after you have planted them.

The best time to dig the soil is in the autumn. It can then stand over winter and the frost, snow and rains will improve its texture greatly. You then plant in the spring. It is never a good plan to plant straight into a newly dug border, the moment you have finished digging it. Heavy rain will cause waterlogging, while strong sunshine will dry the soil out: in either case, you could loose your newly planted shrubs. If you want to plant in the autumn, and that is probably the best time to plant shrubs, then you need to prepare the soil in the spring, and keep it turned during the summer to keep weed growth under control.

**Planting Specimens**

If you want to plant a specimen shrub in the lawn or in a hole in the patio, you still need to prepare the ground properly. For an average type of shrub you need to excavate a circle not less than 4 ft. in diameter, and you need to dig it to a depth of at least 18 in. The procedure is first to remove the turf and put this to one side. Then to remove the topsoil and put that in a separate heap, and finally remove the subsoil, putting that too in a separate heap. The sides of the hole should be vertical, and the bottom of the hole flat. The soil at the bottom of the hole should be loosened, and you then place the sod upside down over the bottom of the hole. The subsoil can then be replaced, mixing it freely with compost or manure.

Preparing a hole for planting a shrub. Note the almost vertical sides of the hole, the flat bottom and the layer of old manure or good compost added to the bottom of the hole to give the plant a good start in its new home.

Finally the topsoil is replaced, improving it if necessary with peat or leaf-mold.


## Weeds

It is particularly important if you are planning a permanent shrubbery to make sure that you have removed all the perennial weeds — things like bindweed, couchgrass and ground elder. If you do not get rid of them completely before you plant, you will never get rid of them, because it will be impossible to deal with them effectively once they become established among your shrubs.

If these weeds are present in the ground you want to turn into a shrubbery the best thing to do is to treat the whole area with a hardhitting non-selective weedkiller. Sodium chlorate, though much maligned, is ideal for this job. It should be applied when the weeds are growing strongly, preferably in spring. A second application may be needed some weeks later if the plants are not killed completely the first time. You need to leave the ground for a good six months after this second application before it is safe to plant. Modern weedkillers such as paraquat are generally not so effective, though may be preferred because it is possible to plant the soil as soon as the weeds are dead.


## When to Plant

Shrubs are normally planted in autumn or spring while they are dormant. They are not, as a rule, planted in the dead of winter, simply because the ground is often unworkable at that time, either because of frost or because of the way soil tends to form heavy, muddy patches after frost or very heavy rains. Tender plants are usually planted in the spring, so that they have a whole summer to grow before having to face their first winter, and one or two shrubs with fleshy roots — such as the magnolias — are best planted early (late April early May) just as they start into growth, so that any roots damaged will heal at once: if planted in autumn such roots may simply rot and ultimately kill the whole shrub.

The great advantage of autumn planting is that the shrubs have the winter rains to settle the soil around their roots: anything planted in the spring is going to need watering, especially as there is almost invariably a dry spell sometime during the summer. In general conifers and evergreens should be planted in spring.

Container grown plants bought from garden centers can be planted at any time of the year, provided care is taken to keep the soil around their roots intact, provided also that the soil is made really firm round the soil ball, and provided still further that they are watered adequately but not to excess during dry periods.

## Planting Intervals

It is very easy to overplant a shrub border, and it is always a shame when this is done, for then the shrubs all run into each other and it is not possible to enjoy the shape and form of each shrub, which is what one wants. To avoid this one needs to plan carefully where each shrub will be located. It is always a help if you have worked this out on paper first — preferably squared graph paper with each square representing a foot.

The counsel of perfection is to find out how big each shrub will grow, and then plant the shrubs so that they will just meet without overgrowing each other. This is not as easy to do as it is to recommend, since the same shrub will grow larger or smaller in different parts of the country, depending on soil, climate and other factors.

The simplest rule is to plant large-growing shrubs 6 ft. apart, medium-sized shrubs 3 ft. apart, and small shrubs 18 in. to 2 ft. apart — but if you use small shrubs plant them in groups of 3 or 5, rather than singly: they will be far more effective.

If you follow this advice, when you unbend your back from planting, you may find that the border looks very bare. Don't worry, if you have done your groundwork properly, in a season or two the shrubs will already start to fill out and occupy the space allotted to them. Meanwhile, you can fill the gaps with bedding plants or bulbs, or work out some ground-cover scheme which can be of permanent value.

## Planting

Unless you buy your shrubs only from a garden center, the chances are that they will arrive by mail, neatly packed.

Once you've got your package unwrap it in the garage or garden shed. The first thing to do is to check all the labels to make sure they bear the names of all the plants you ordered. Assuming that they do, you should then examine the shrubs to make sure, to the best of your ability, that the shrubs actually are what their labels claim them to be. Very few nurserymen ever send out shrubs wrongly labelled deliberately, but mistakes do happen. If you think you have been sent the wrong plant, replacement may be possible if you write the nurseryman without delay.

The next thing to do is to see whether the shrubs have become unduly dry during their journey. If they have place them in a bucket of water for a couple of hours. Often you will not need to do this.

Next examine the shrubs critically. Usually you will find that a few roots are broken or damaged due to lifting at the nursery. Damaged roots do not heal well, and can give a shrub a considerable set-back. Any damaged roots should be pruned cleanly away, so that the cut surface will face downwards once the shrub is planted. A clean cut like this will heal quickly, giving the shrub little set-back.

◀ *Magnolia* 'Dr. Merrill', one of the superb new hybrids.

*Hydrangea paniculata.*
Most spectacular when cut back hard each year: it will then produce flower heads 18 inches long. ▶

*Hibiscus syriacus,* Shrub althea, one of the few late-summer flowering shrubs. ▼

Having examined the roots for positive damage, the next thing to do is to examine the whole shrub. What you are looking for is a balance between top growth and root growth. If roots have been left behind in the soil when the shrub was lifted, you will have to remove some top growth to balance this. As a general principal it is always worth removing some of the top growth when planting new shrubs, and with deciduous shrubs it is usually recommended that they should be cut back by about one third of their size. Conifers and evergreens, both of which usually arrive with their roots balled (that is in a ball of soil covered with burlap) do not need this pruning. If, however, you do find evergreens that have had their roots damaged, pick a proportion of the leaves off the plant — as much as half the leaves if the damage is severe. The problem with evergreens — both conifers and broadleaved—is that the leaves go on giving off moisture all through the winter, and if they give off more moisture than the roots can absorb, then they die of drought. Cold winds cause them to give off more moisture than usual, and if the ground gets frozen really hard that can lock up all the free water, and that too can cause young evergreens to die of drought. It is always worth protecting newly planted evergreens from cold winds with a temporary screen of burlap.

If you do not have the time to plant the shrubs on arrival, or if you have not completed preparing the ground, they should be heeled in until you are ready. This is done by taking out a shallow, V-shaped trench and putting the plants obliquely into it. They are then easily lifted when you are ready to plant them.

When it comes to the actual planting there are two roles of tremendous importance. The first is that the hole that is made in the already prepared soil should be sufficiently large to accommodate all the roots of the shrub without any of them having to be cramped or folded to get them in. The other is that the shrub should be planted to precisely the same depth in the soil as it was in the nursery: if it is planted deeper soil will cover part of the main stem that was never meant to be underground, and this will rot and the shrub will die. It is better to err on the side of planting the shrub too high if in doubt.

Having opened up the hole, hold the shrub over it to make sure that all its roots will fit in easily. From there you really need two people, one holding the shrub at its correct planting height, the other filling in with soil. The soil should be returned around the roots in layers about 3 or 4 in. thick and each layer should be firmed. The easiest way of making sure that the planting level will be correct is to lay a board across the hole, since this will show you where your soil will reach once the hole has been filled in. After filling and firming, the shrub should be watered, and this is more important with evergreen than with deciduous shrubs, but it should be done for both. Evergreens should have their foliage sprayed, as well as having their roots watered. Any shrub more than 6 or 9 in. high should be securely tied to a stout cane to prevent it rocking loose in the wind. This is particularly liable to happen to evergreens which, since they retain their leaves all winter, offer enough resistance to wind to really rock themselves loose.

**Aftercare**
Once shrubs have been planted they need a little care and affection to get them established quickly. There are two important rules here, which may at first seem contradictory. The first is to keep the soil around the shrub clean of weeds: the second is not to disturb the soil around the newly planted shrubs. In fact this is quite easily achieved by mulching, either with leaf-mold or peat, both of which are equally effective. Mulching not only suppresses all weeds, it also helps to prevent the moisture in the soil from evaporating too fast. The mulch should be 2 or 3 in. thick, and care should be taken that it does not close in around the collar of the plant: if it does it will have exactly the same effect as planting the shrub too deep in the first place. Birds are very inclined to scavenge through a mulch, and you should check periodically to see that they have not thrown the mulch up around the stems of the shrubs. It is well worth adding a second mulch during mid-summer, to suppress any seedling weeds that may be emerging.

If weeds do prove a problem they can most easily be controlled by applying one of the pre-emergence weedkillers based on simazine. These are highly effective and do the shrubs no damage. To work really well they need to be applied as soon as the shrubs have been planted. Another application should be made around mid-summer. Any weeds that do manage to appear can easily be removed by hand: they will just lift out of the mulch.

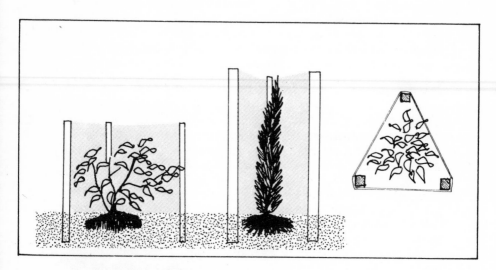

Protecting a newly planted
evergreen from winter winds. It is
the cold winds from the north and
east that usually kill young
evergreens, rather than sheer
degrees of cold. Three stout stakes
are inserted in the ground and
burlap nailed to these
on two sides.

Staking a young shrub. This is
particularly important in the case of
evergreens, the example shown here
being a camellia. Unless staked
wind can cause the young shrubs
to sway, and this in turn can prevent
the roots from becoming established.

# 5 Pruning

There are two ways of pruning shrubs: the right way and the wrong way, and of the two the second is by far the more commonly practiced. It consists basically of going out with a pair of pruning shears and removing branches from your shrubs because some inner urge tells you that it might be a good idea to do so. Such pruning may satisfy an inner urge, but it will do the shrubs no good.

The right way to prune a shrub is to take note of whether it flowers on wood of the current season's growth, or on wood of the previous season's growth. This is easily established simply by examining the plant when in flower. If it flowers on wood of the current season's growth (and this includes most of the shrubs which flower after mid-summer), the shoots that have flowered are cut back hard in spring before growth starts, to encourage plenty of new growth. If it flowers on wood of the previous season's growth (and this includes most of the shrubs which flower in spring and early summer), then the whole shoot which has flowered should be cut out immediately after flowering, sometimes right down to ground level.

When pruning it is always worth remembering *why* one is pruning. The purpose of pruning is to promote the production of healthy flowering or fruiting wood. It may also serve the additional purpose of keeping the shrub tidy.

It would be quite wrong to think that all shrubs need pruning, and must fit into one or other of the two categories described above. The simple fact is that the great majority of shrubs seldom need pruning at all.

There is one operation sometimes described as pruning, though it scarcely amounts to that, called dead-heading. This simply involves removing the dead flower heads once the flowers are over. In the case of rhododendrons this is simply done by picking the trusses off between thumb and finger, but with lilacs and many other shrubs this needs to be done with shears. The purpose of dead-heading is to prevent the shrub

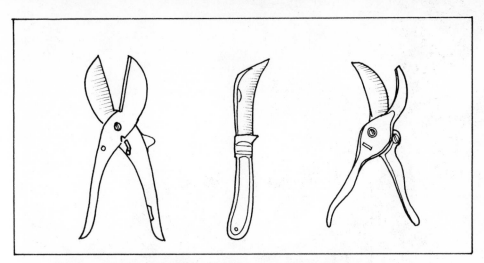

Pruning tools. Though there are dozens of different pruning tools on the market, the ones shown here are all one normally needs. Left, anvil type pruning shears, center, a pruning knife and, right, the parrot's beak type of pruning shears.

Pruning cuts. Left, the cut correctly made: center, the cut made too close to the bud which will cause the wood to die back to the bud below and, right, the cut made too high above the bud, which will result in that wood dying back to the bud. Any die-back caused by incorrect pruning produces dead wood that is a focus for infection that could kill the whole plant.

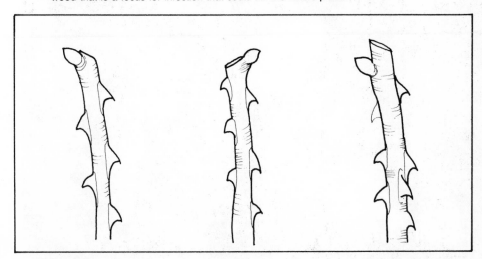

This is what is meant by pruning hard. It results in very vigorous new growth. Used mostly for plants grown for the bright colors of their young twigs.

Loppers are useful tools for pruning shoots that are too thick for shears to cope with.

Pruning an evergreen: always use shears and take care not to cut through the leaves: cutting the leaves will cause them to brown.

from putting its energies into producing unwanted seeds, which would diminish its crop of flowers the following year. It is always worth dead-heading any shrub for which this treatment is recommended. You need only dead-head one side of a rhododendron and leave the other half with its dead flowers on to see the difference this makes in the following year.

As for tools for pruning, one does not need a great armory of weapons. All that one needs is a good pair of shears. There are two basic types of shears on the market — though there are several variations on both themes — the parrot-bill type and the anvil type. With the parrot-bill type the blades cut by crossing each other: with the anvil type the cut is made by one blade closing against a flat surface. It really does not matter which you have: what does matter is that they are sharp. The cost of having them sharpened is very small, and well worth while. Blunt shears do endless damage. Like all good tools, shears should be treated with respect: never try to cut anything that is too big for them to cut easily, and never twist the shears while cutting.

Suckers are a ready means of increasing any shrub that has a suckering habit.

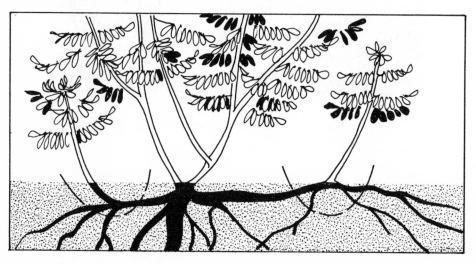

# 6 Propagating Shrubs

It is the creativeness of increasing plants that makes it such fun — sometimes so much of a challenge, and so rewarding when one is successful. Certainly most keen gardeners increase their plants just for the fun of it, but it has a useful function too. If you have a shrub that you think is really outstanding and you want three more of it, rather than buy them, try propagating them yourself: you will be far more satisfied with the results. You may also find that other people are often asking for a piece of one of your shrubs: try propagating it yourself, then you'll have the pleasure of being able to give pieces away: you may even find other people who enjoy increasing their plants, and then you will be able to swap one good thing for another.

The great majority of shrubs are quite easy to increase. Unfortunately, the more difficult they are to increase the more expensive they are to buy, and in many ways one would gain most by being able to increase the difficult ones. That will come with practice.

There are four main ways in which shrubs are increased: by seed, by cutting, by layering and by grafting. Of these grafting is used only for a rather small number of shrubs such as the tree peony *Paeonia suffruticosa* and many roses. It is too much of a specialized subject to cover here, and any enthusiast should read a good book on propagation which covers that as well as all other aspects of plant propagation in more detail.

### Seed
This is the easiest and cheapest way of increasing shrubs, and it is surprising just how many shrubs can be increased in this way: it is also surprising just how young some of them will flower — many in their third year from seed. Indeed, anyone planning a shrub garden on a shoestring would do well to consider the idea of growing all he can from seed.

Yet if one is growing shrubs from seed one must be aware of the problems. Species will in general come true from seed, but hybrids and sports

Layering *Magnolia stellata*, an operation that should be carried out early in spring just as the sap is rising but before the buds have burst.

Layering a rhododendron.

will not. If you don't know that you may well be very disappointed by the results. Thus, for example, if you sow seed of a named variety of almost any shrub you should expect the seedlings to be inferior to it and more like the botanical type plant. If you sow seed of a variegated shrub, do not expect the seedlings to be variegated: it is highly unlikely that they will be. And if you sow seed of a hybrid, the resulting seedlings will almost certainly be different from the hybrid from which you obtained the seed, a proportion reverting to one parent, and a proportion reverting to the other parent. The chances of your getting something even better are possible but negligible.

If you don't know the difference between a true species, a variety and a hybrid you are obviously going to run into problems, so it is worth explaining them. The naming of plants is the easiest way to recognize these differences. A species is a plant that bears two names, both in Latin, always (if correctly) written in italics, the initial letter of the first name being capitalized. Thus *Cornus florida* is a species. *Cornus florida* 'Rubra', on the other hand, is a variety, the varietal name being written in single quotes and in roman lettering. Alternatively, varieties may be written *Cornus florida* var. 'Rubra'. Hybrids are invariably distinguished by a hybrid sign, viz. ×, somewhere in their name. Thus *Cornus* × 'Eddy's White Wonder', is plainly a hybrid, and this is how you will find most hybrid plant names written. It is, however, a named form. What happened was that someone crossed *Cornus florida* with *Cornus nuttallii:* that cross is simply written *Cornus florida* × *nuttallii,* and all the seedlings of that cross, made by anyone anywhere at any time would be written that way and would belong to what is known as a grex. An outstanding seedling from that cross, selected and named, such as 'Eddy's White Wonder', is known as a clone and can only be increased vegetatively — that is by cuttings, layers or grafting. All this, of course, is fine so long as you keep all your plants clearly labelled, or obtain your seed from clearly labelled plants. But if you just take seed from an unnamed plant that happens to take your fancy, the results may surprise you!

It is not only hybrids and varieties that will not come true from seed. Sometimes species cannot be relied upon to come true from seed. This applies really to only a limited number of genera, among the most notorious of which are the rose, the barberries, the cotoneasters and the maples.

Seed is not really to be advised for anyone in a hurry. Many shrub seeds take about two years to germinate, and some can take as long as four years. Roughly speaking, the smaller the seed the faster it will germinate; the larger the seed the longer it will take. Small seeds will usually germinate within a couple of months or never: it is the large seeds that will keep you waiting — and even then they just may disappoint you by not coming up at all.

With many hardy shrubs the seed can be sown in the open ground where it will germinate satisfactorily. This is, however, not really the best way of going about raising shrubs from seed. The best practice is to sow the seed in pots, which can be clearly labelled, and which can moreover be gathered together in one part of the garden, possibly in a frame if you have one, where they can more easily be protected from birds, mice, rabbits and other animals that have the irritating habit of digging them up or eating them.

Pots should be properly crocked with bits of broken pot placed over the hole at the bottom — and clay pots are generally preferred over plastic pots for seed that is to be grown out of doors because they are porous — and some course peat placed over the crocks to prevent fine soil getting washed down into the crocks and damming up the drainage. For fine seed it is worth using a soil-based potting mixture screened every fine, but for larger seeds any good garden soil, well sifted, will do. Seeds should be covered to roughly their own depth with soil, and firmed well. Once this has been done the soil or compost should come to within about ½ in. of the top of the pot. The pot should then be plunged to the rim in soil or sand, watered well and covered first with a piece of glass and then with some brown paper: the point of the glass and brown paper is to prevent evaporation and to keep the soil constantly and evenly moist. Once the seeds have germinated the brown paper should be removed, and this should be done as soon as possible after germination, for the seeds will then need light to keep growing. If they are kept in the dark they will quickly become ''leggy'' and fall prey to diseases. Any seeds that need more than a year to germinate will need frost to break their dormancy — so don't be tempted to move them into the warmth of a greenhouse: leave them out and let the frost do its work. Seed of tender shrubs, on the other hand, will often need some warmth to get it to germinate.

Once the seedlings have germinated and are large enough to handle, prick them off into larger containers. In the case of plants of the pea family — plants like the brooms, the Judas tree or the laburnum — prick the seedlings out individually: they resent root disturbance and should be planted in their permanent positions as soon as they are large enough to survive there. If you have a frame it is useful to grow the seedlings in it until they are well established little plants.

### Cuttings
Cuttings are the most commonly used of all methods of increasing shrubs. There are, however, three different types of cuttings used, and, although many books will tell you that you use one type for one shrub and another type for another shrub, in practice it does not always work out quite as simply as that: for one thing, it takes judgement to tell at precisely

which moment the cutting itself is ready to be taken. The general rule, if in doubt as to which type of cutting to take, is to try softwood cuttings first, then half-ripe cuttings and finally hardwood cuttings — as the three different types are called — in that order.

SOFTWOOD CUTTINGS   These are cuttings taken from the growing tip of the shoots and trimmed just below a node (a node is the point at which leaves occur on the shoot). The best time to take cuttings of this type is during May and June, which will give well-established plants by autumn. Alternatively some shrubs can be increased by cuttings of this type taken in September — but these will need to be seen through the winter in the safety of a greenhouse.

The easiest way of taking the cuttings is to remove them from the parent plant with a 'heel' (a piece of the old wood) by pulling downwards and outwards. The cutting can then be trimmed with a new razor blade below the node, and dipped in root promoting or hormone rooting powder. Care should be taken in the use of these rooting powders: if used discreetly they seem to help rooting, but if used in excess they may retard it. The cuttings should then be inserted around the edge of a pot, each cutting being slipped into a small hole made with a dibble in the compost, and then well firmed. It is important to ensure that the bottom of the cutting and all the parts below the surface of the soil are in contact with the soil, and this is done by pushing the dibble down into the soil beside the cutting.

The great problem with softwood cuttings is simply that they are soft: the wood has not hardened, and indeed the leaves are still limp, and the cutting is therefore liable to wilt. To prevent this it needs to be kept under humid conditions, either in a frame in the garden or in a plastic propagating case which consists of an opaque plastic base in which you stand the pots of cuttings, and a clear plastic dome. While these conditions must be attained if the cutting is to root before it wilts, they are also the ideal conditions for many fungal diseases, and the cuttings should be sprayed weekly with a fungicide to prevent the occurrence of fungus growth. If you have neither a frame nor a propagating case many cuttings of this type can be rooted successfully if the whole pot, cuttings and all, is wrapped in a plastic bag and sealed with sticky-tape.

HALF-RIPE CUTTINGS   Cuttings of this type are generally easier to handle than softwood cuttings, since they are less liable to wilt. However, although the base of the cutting — the part which will root — may have

Soft tip cuttings being taken below a node, right. Top left, the cutting showing what needs to be done to prepare it for planting and, bottom left, the prepared cutting ready for inserting in the rooting medium.

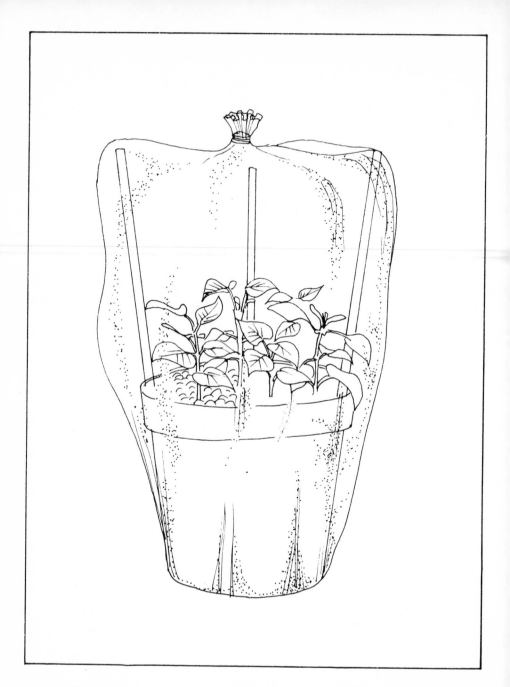

Rooting is better when the relative humidity
is high. Covering the pot and cuttings in a
plastic bag helps.

become woody, the growing end may still be growing, and may still be soft enough to wilt, so some care is still needed in their handling.

Half-ripe cuttings are taken between June and September and are *always* taken with a heel. This is most easily achieved by pushing your thumb firmly into the angle between the new growth (the cutting) and the old wood. The cutting will come away with quite a large piece of the old wood and old bark attached to it. The heel needs to be trimmed with a razor blade to get rid of the loose bark and to give it a clean, flat face: it should not simply be planted straight from the shrub without this tidying up.

The cutting needs further preparing before it can be planted. Any soft extension growth should be trimmed off, and all the leaves should also be removed, taking care when this is done that the leaf-stalk stumps are not left behind, and that the soft new bark is not torn away when the leaves are removed. The finished cutting will usually be between four and six inches long.

It is then planted and grown in exactly the same way as a softwood cutting, except that it does not require such humid conditions.

HARDWOOD CUTTINGS   These are the easiest of all cuttings to take, but not necessarily the easiest to grow. A hardwood cutting consists simply of a shoot of bare wood taken in autumn and inserted into an area of pre-pared soil in the open garden. The cuttings are usually about a foot long, and may be taken either with a heel or trimmed to a node. They should be buried to two-thirds of their length in the soil, and are best laid in a V-shaped trench along the bottom of which some coarse sand has been placed. The soil is then returned and the cuttings made firm. They need to be refirmed in the soil after any and every frost, since these will tend to loosen them in the ground. They will form a callus during the winter, and root in spring as growth begins.

All this is easy enough, but it is also very easy to lose the cuttings in spring, for there is all too often a dry, sunny period just as the leaf buds begin to expand, and the expansion of the leaf buds occurs just before the cuttings begin to send out roots — so that at that time they do not have any roots with which to absorb moisture to support their leaves. They there-fore need plenty of watering until obviously self-sufficient, which is not usually until early summer. By autumn they will be well rooted and can then be moved.

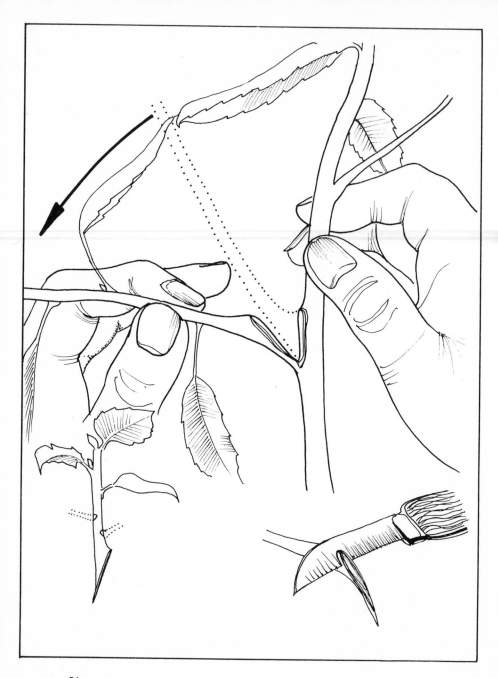

## Layering

Almost any shrub whose branches can be brought down to the ground can be increased by layering. The operation is a very simple one. First you bend the branch down so that it is parallel with the ground: you then put a peg or two into the ground to hold it in that position. Next you hollow out a small hole in the ground, adding some sand to the soil at the bottom of

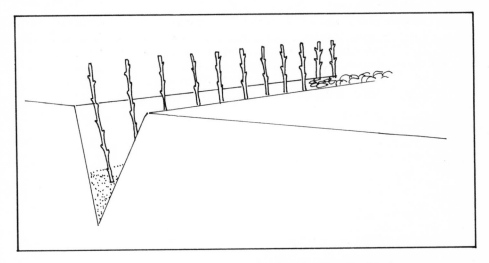

Hardwood cuttings lined up in a V-shaped trench at the bottom of which has been placed some sharp sand. The next step is to fill the trench with loose soil.

Half-ripe cuttings being taken with a heel: this is done by pulling the cuttings downwards and outwards from the old wood of the shrub. Bottom left, the cuttings with the lower leaves removed. Bottom right, the base of the cutting trimmed and ready for planting.

55

the hole. You then bend the twig down into the hole and peg it into position. Next, refill the hole with soil and tie the growing tip of the twig securely to a cane or stick. Finally, water the ground in which the shoot has been buried, and place a flat stone over it to prevent moisture from evaporating too fast. Leave well alone until rooted — which will usually take two years for the new plant to be well-enough established to move.

The best time of year to carry out layering is mid-summer, but it can be done at almost any time. The best wood to use is year old wood, and the point at which new growth emerges from this is one of the likeliest places for rooting to occur.

Some plants need a little assistance in rooting when layered, and almost anything that will constrict the flow of sap through the layer will help. This can be done by either making a slit in the wood to about half its thickness, or by removing a narrow band of bark from the lower half of the stem at the point at which the most acute bending will occur underground. Roots will then form immediately below this point.

Layering, one of the easiest methods of increasing shrubs. The picture on the right shows a suitable branch pegged in the ground. The small drawing on the left shows a portion of bark removed to encourage rooting.

# 7 Deciduous Shrubs

Deciduous shrubs are those that lose their leaves in winter. All such shrubs come from parts of the world that have differentiated seasons, which means in effect cold winters and less cold summers. They come from climates that are as cold in winter as our northern states, or often even colder, and the great majority of them can be relied upon as being completely hardy. There are few exceptions, notably the fuschias and the hydrangeas, both of which are safest given a little protection in the winter.

## *Acer*/Maples

These are grown not for their flowers, which are seldom noticed, but for their foliage and their usually brilliant autumn coloring. They all grow best in sheltered positions in good, moist well-drained soil, with preferably a little shade. *A. japonicum* 'Aureum', 4 ft. by 4 ft., slow growing with beautiful soft yellow lobed leaves which are exceptional among yellow leaved deciduous shrubs in that they hold their color throughout the summer. *A. japonicum* 'Laciniatum' ('Filicifolium'), 6 ft. by 5 ft., leaves deeply lobed and toothed, green, turning brilliant scarlet in autumn, slow growing but eventually a tall shrub or small tree. *A. palmatum,* 12 ft. to 15 ft., the Japanese maple, slow growing, ultimately forming a small tree, leaves lobed, coloring brilliantly in autumn. *A. palmatum* 'Atropurpureum', slower growing, 6 ft. by 4 ft., leaves purple, turning bright crimson when seen against the light, superb autumn color. *A. palmatum* 'Dissectum', 2 ft. by 4 ft., forms a low-growing mushroom-shaped shrub, leaves very finely divided, fresh green turning bright orange in autumn, dislikes cold winds. 'Dissectum Atropurpureum' is a form with purple leaves, the two look exceptionally good when planted together. *A. heptalobum* 'Osakazuki', 5 ft. by 5 ft., leaves large, lobed, green providing some of the most brilliant autumn color of any shrub, passing through every shade of yellow, orange, scarlet and crimson.

## Aralia

Not really trees at all, but growing to 10 ft., and usually suckering mildly, these shrubs are grown for their huge tripinnate leaves which can be over 3 ft. long and for their enormous plumes of white flowers borne in August/September. Wood is soft and easily damaged by frosts, but this seldom kills the plants. The green leaved form *A. chinensis* is not particularly good; infinitely better are *A. chinensis* 'Aurea Marginata' and *A. chinensis* 'Argentea Marginata' which have gold and silver variegations respectively and are among the finest of all variegated shrubs. Sandy soil. Division, grafting.

## Artemesia

Known variously as lad's love, southernwood or old man, the most shrubby of the family is *A. abrotanum* which is grown primarily for its silvery-grey, finely divided feathery foliage — like lace. Usually rather untidy, becomes a neat, rounded dome if cut hard down each spring, 3 ft. by 4 ft. *A. arborescens* is similar and has even finer silver foliage, 4 ft. by 4 ft. Hardwood cuttings. Put these in the ground where you want them to grow.

## Azalea

Properly these belong in the genus *Rhododendron,* but the term azalea is generally taken to mean all the deciduous members of the family, together with a race of plants popularly known as the dwarf Japanese azaleas. All need acid soil, a cool, moist soil and plenty of peat and

The dwarf Japanese cut-leaf maple *Acer palmatum* 'Dissectum' is one of the most showy of all shrubs grown for their autumn color.

Dwarf broom, *Cytisus praecox,* makes a low mound of primrose yellow flowers in spring.

leaf-mold mixed into the soil. Most do best in light shade. No pruning needed, but it pays to dead-head after flowering — except with the dwarf evergreen types, which seldom set seed.

**Deciduous** There are literally hundreds of named varieties and it is impossible to describe them all. They are, however, divided into four main groups, each with its own characteristics. These are:

GHENT azaleas, which flower in May and have a remarkably strong scent, flowers single or double, not very large.

MOLLIS azaleas, which flower about two weeks earlier, have no scent, do not grow so tall but have larger flowers and most have good autumn color.

KNAPHILL azaleas, an improvement on the above two types, being the result mainly of crossing the Ghent and Mollis types, they combine the best of both types, with larger flowers and wider range of colors.

EXBURY azaleas, the finest and also the most expensive of all, with huge flowers and an enormous range of colors, usually very vibrant, plus the bonus of good autumn color. Also beginning to appear on the market are the:

WINDSOR azaleas, which have been derived from the Exbury azaleas but are even better. Both the last two can be bought either as named plants (the most expensive way), or as seedlings true to color (which is cheaper) or else simply as unflowered seedlings. Cheapest of all is simply to buy seed, the seedlings are invariably good. Colors range from purest white through every shade of pink and orange to brightest scarlet and deep crimson.

**Evergreen azaleas** These are mainly low-growing, mound-forming plants with tiny leaves and large flowers; the flowers are produced so freely that they literally hide the foliage. Again, there are too many to give a comprehensive list, but among the best are: 'Palestrina', purest white with a hint of green and a very useful foil to the pinks or for separating the pinks from other shades; 'Leo', bright orange, huge flowers, spreading habit, good ground cover; 'John Cairns', the best deep red; 'Hinomayo', the finest pure pink, small flowers but masses of them; 'Mother's Day', very large deep pink flowers; 'Vuyk's Rosy-red', huge shot-silk pink flowers. All are excellent at the front of the border, but most need shade because the flowers tend to fade in sunlight.

## *Berberis*/Barberries

See also Evergreen Shrubs. A large charming group of both deciduous and evergreen shrubs, all of which are very easy to grow in any soil. All are very spiny. What you finish up with may well depend upon what your local garden center happens to offer, but the following are among the best deciduous species. *B.* × *rubrostilla,* 6 ft. by 4 ft., one of the very best, flowers yellow in short panicles in May/June, leaves small, pale green; in autumn the arching branches are covered with masses of fruits varying from white to carmine. *B. thunbergii,* 5 ft. by 1½ ft., small prickly leaves, straw-colored flowers May/June, and bright red berries and leaves in autumn. *B. thunbergii* 'Atropurpurea' has rich bronzy-red foliage which turns rich red in autumn: a highly effective foliage contrast plant, *B. wilsoniae,* 3 ft. by 4 ft., is very spiny; the flowers are a rather dull yellow May/June, followed by great ropes of glowing coral berries in autumn. The leaves are soft, small, and turn red and orange in autumn. Increase by seed, but seedlings may be variable. Half-ripe cuttings are safer.

## *Buddleia*/Butterfly bush

Fast-growing shrubs valued for their summer flowers, grow well in any soil but preferring a sunny site. The ever-popular butterfly bush is *B. davidii,* to 15 ft., producing dense spikes of purplish flowers in July/ August. The darkest is 'Black Knight', 'Fascination' has huge spikes of lilac-pink flowers while 'Peace' has very large heads of pure white flowers. 'Harlequin' has reddish-purple flowers and leaves strikingly variegated creamy-white. Prune hard early each spring, cutting right back to the last pair of buds on each of the previous season's shoots. *B. alternifolia,* 15 ft. by 15 ft., is very different in appearance, producing lilac-mauve flowers in clusters all along the backs of the arching twigs through June and July. It has small, willow-shaped leaves, and a stronger scent than any other buddleia. Flowers quite well when left unpruned but is even better when shoots that have flowered are removed immediately after flowering. Half-ripe cuttings.

## Californian tree poppy: see *Romneya*

## *Caryopteris*/Blue spirea

Only one species, *C. incana,* is grown. 4 ft. by 4 ft. A grey-leaved shrub prized for its pure blue flowers borne in terminal spikes from August till October. Best grown in groups, and makes an ideal partner for fuschias. Needs full sun and well drained soil, and may get killed in a hard winter, especially if the ground gets very wet. Prune hard in April to the last pair of buds on the previous season's growth. Soft cuttings in May or hardwood cuttings in October or November.

## *Callicarpa*/Beauty-berry

Uncommon shrubs grown for their unusual berries and equally unusual autumn foliage. *C. Giraldiana,* 7 ft. by 4 ft., leaves and stems downy, pale pink flowers August, autumn color pink and mauve, the bare branches covered in bright violet berries. The variety 'Profusion' bears an even heavier crop of berries. Seed; hardwood cuttings.

## *Ceanothus*/Californian lilac

The deciduous ceanothus are far hardier than the evergreen ones, but never achieve that richness of blue for which this genus is famed, the flowers being a rather muddy color. The two best are 'Gloire de Versailles' with sky blue flowers, and 'Topaz', with slightly deeper blue flowers. 5 ft. by 5 ft. Prune back hard to within two buds of the last season's growth each spring. Flowers are produced in large trusses from June till autumn, with two main flushes. Soft cuttings in June; hardwood cuttings, October.

## *Ceratostigma*/Plumbago

One species, *C. willmottianum,* is grown for its very pure blue flowers produced from August until the frosts. It mixes well with fuschias and the shrubby potentillas. 3 ft., usually less. It is only semi-woody, and the winter's frosts will usually kill it back to ground level or near ground level. Division or half-ripe cuttings.

## *Chaenomeles*/Flowering quince

Known to countless generations of gardeners simply as 'Japonica', it is one of those annoying plants whose names are constantly being changed by botanists. It has been known variously as Pyrus, Cydonia and more recently as *Chaenomeles lagenaria* but is now *Chaenomeles speciosa.*

Universally known simply as 'Japonica', the flowering quince *Chaenomeles speciosa* is a highly effective flowering shrub. It is available in a wide range of colors.

Under whatever name it is a good garden shrub with a dense, tangled habit of growth. Shy flowering when young, it soon settles down to putting up a good show every year. It flowers most freely in full sun. In a sheltered position it will start flowering in January, building up to its best in April. Vigorous forms grow up to 10 ft. 'Knaphill Scarlet' is one of the brightest and best; 'Rosea Flore Pleno' has double pink flowers; 'Apple Blossom' has good large pale pink flowers. Suckers or layers.

## *Chimonanthus*/Wintersweet

*C. praecox* is one of the most delightful of winter flowering shrubs, producing its pale yellow, scarlet-throated flowers from November till February. The scent is perhaps even more marvellous than the flowers. Leaves large, bright green turning yellow in autumn. Young plants take time to settle down to flowering. 10 ft. by 6 ft. Shorten shoots that have flowered immediately after flowering. Seed or layers.

## *Chionanthus*/Fringe tree

Seldom tree like, *C. virginicus* is grown for its drooping fringe-like panicles of scented white flowers which are borne June/July, but only on established plants. Leaves long, pointed, turning yellow in autumn. 10 ft. by 8 ft. Seed.

## *Cotinus*/Smoke tree

Sometimes included under *Rhus,* these are quite distinct, with oval or round leaves, and great loose flower-heads. 10 ft. by 8 ft. Any soil, preferably sun. *C. coggygria* flowers so freely that the whole plant appears to be hidden in a haze of smoke. Brilliant orange and scarlet autumn color. The variety 'Atropurpurea' differs in having purple stems to the flowers and in the leaves turning yellow in autumn. 'Notcutt's Variety' has superb rich purple foliage which turns clear claret when seen against the sun; the flowers are purple and pink. By far the most effective. Layers; hardwood cuttings.

## *Cornus*/Dogwood

A large family and a very mixed bunch. Some are grown for their winter bark, some for their variegated leaves and some for their flowers.
**For bark** There are two outstanding species, *C. alba* produces the brightest red young shoots of any shrub — and is most useful in its variegated form 'Spaethii', with golden splashed leaves; 'Elegantissima' has leaves variegated silver and is just as effective. For contrast plant *C. stolonifera* 'Flaviramea' which has brilliant yellow young stems. To get the best coloring on the young stems, cut the plants back hard to old wood just as the new leaves are emerging in March. Both plants will grow in very boggy conditions, literally with their roots in the water.

**For variegation** *C. alternifolia* 'Variegata' is one of the finest of all variegated shrubs, with small leaves richly marked with white. It has a neat twiggy habit, and needs no pruning. 10 ft. by 6 ft.

**For flower** The Cornelian cherry, *C. mas,* is useful for its abundance of small yellow flowers in February. These are followed by red oval fruits. There are three variegated forms, all good: 'Aurea', variegated gold; 'Tricolor', variegated yellow and pink; and 'Variegata', leaves margined white. The Cornelian cherry produces a good autumn color on poor soil.

The other flowering dogwoods are very different. The flower is a cluster of tiny, insignificant stamens, but this is surrounded by large, showy bracts (modified leaves which are colored and look like petals). Of these the most reliable is *C. kousa,* with pointed white bracts which slowly turn pink, produced during May/June and lasting a good six weeks. *C. kousa chinensis* has even larger bracts. Curious red raspberry-like fruits are produced in late summer, and autumn color is good on good soils. Mature plants develop a tiered habit, with flat, tabulated branches upon which the flowers appear to dance, held upright on long stalks. Slow growing to 15 ft. by 10 ft. *C. nuttallii* is even finer, with larger bracts as much as 3 in. long and delicate pink autumn coloring, but it needs an acid soil and a sheltered position. *C. florida* is similar to *C. kousa* and is native to the eastern states; the bracts are twisted in a curious manner. *C. florida* 'Rubra' has pink bracts and is even better. The wood needs a good ripening if the shrub is to flower well. 12 ft. by 8 ft. No pruning for any of the flowering dogwoods. Increase by seed or hardwood cuttings.

# *Corylopsis*/Winter Hazel

Another of those treasures with yellow, scented flowers produced very early in the year, any time from December to February. *C. spicata* is generally the best species to grow, producing short hanging spikes of pale primrose open bell-shaped flowers. 4 ft. by 5 ft. Prefers the shelter of other shrubs, and needs a lime-free soil. Leaves hazel-like. No pruning. Layers.

# *Corylus*/Hazels

*C. avellana* 'Contorta', known as Harry Lauder's Walking Stick', is a curious form with curiously curled and twisted branches, useful for floral decoration. 10 ft. by 10 ft. *C. maxima* 'Purpurea', the purple hazelnut has large typically hazel leaves of a singularly deep, rich purple color and purple catkins in spring. One of the most dramatic of all purple shrubs; looks best contrasted with a yellow-leaved or variegated shrub, preferably evergreen for contrast. Prune really hard each spring. Hardwood cuttings.

## Cotoneaster

A huge family, the best known of which is the herring-bone cotoneaster, *C. horizantalis,* which produces its branches in flat, fish-bone design; if grown against a wall these will press themselves flat against it. It also makes a good ground-cover plant. Leaves tiny, almost round, turning crimson in autumn; masses of bright red berries. The form 'Variegatus' has prettily variegated leaves and is more effective. *C. dammeri* is a ground-hugging species producing cherry-sized crimson fruits in autumn and into winter. Layers, seed, hardwood cuttings.

## *Cytisus*/Broom

See also *Genista spartium.* Colorful but short-lived shrubs, useful for planting in a new garden to give instant effect until the permanent members of the shrubbery are established, after which they can be discarded. They hate root disturbance and once planted should never be moved. Tend to suffer from wind-rock. Any necessary pruning should be done after flowering. All have green twigs, minute but deciduous leaves and pea-type flowers. The hybrids grow 7 ft. by 5 ft.: × *burkwoodii,* masses of maroon and red flowers; 'Killiney Salmon', flowers orange; 'Newry Seedling', red and cream flowers; 'Cornish Cream', flowers ivory and pale yellow. Of the smaller growing plants *C. praecox* is one of the best, 5 ft. by 5 ft., producing in May masses of pale primrose flowers. *C.* × *kewensis* is one of the best dwarfs for the front of a border, 1½ ft. by 4 ft., sulphur-yellow flowers April/May. *C. purpureus incarnatus,* 2 ft. by 4 ft., produces soft mauve flowers in June/July. Increase by seed or half-ripe cuttings taken in June-August. Not always easy to root.

## *Daphne*

Grown primarily for their tremendous fragrance, the daphnes mentioned here are all hardy but a bit temperamental. Grow best in an open, sunny location. Easily increased and replaced. *D. mezereum,* the mezereon, a British native, stiff-erect twigs smothered in February/March with purplish red or lilac flowers, very strongly scented. Var. 'Album' has pure white flowers and makes an effective contrast. Its berries are yellow, those of the type plant red. Both form a ready means of increase, but you must bury them before the birds get them. Leaves small. Good at the front of the border, and best planted in groups. *D.* 'Somerset' (× *burkwoodii*), 3 ft. by 3 ft., forms a dense, dome-shaped bush covered in May with very sweetly scented soft mauve-pink flowers. Half-ripe cuttings.

## *Decaisnea fargesii*

Grown primarily for its brilliant turquoise inflated seed pods, this is an unusual and striking shrub, with large, pinnate leaves a foot long and yellow, pea-type flowers in spring. It forms a tall shrub to 10 ft. by 3 ft., consisting of numerous erect stems. Rich soil. Seed. Plants not generally available.

Deutzias are among the most popular of flowering shrubs. Many are very large growing: see text for types recommended for smaller gardens.

## Deutzia

A very easily grown family of thoroughly reliable June-flowering shrubs. All produce erect stems and clusters of small flowers, usually white, occasionally pink. Any soil, sun or slight shade. *D. gracilis,* 3 ft. by 3 ft., densely twiggy, numerous white flowers; *D. discolor* × *elegantissima,* 5 ft. by 4 ft., scented, rose-tinted flowers; 'Magician', 6 ft. by 4 ft., rich rose flowers, superb; 'Campanulata', 5 ft. by 3 ft., flowers purest white; *D. scabra* 'Pride of Rochester', 7 ft. by 4 ft., double white. Prune out flowering wood right after flowering right back to where new growths have started. Half-ripe cuttings taken after flowering.

## Eucryphia

Only one member of this genus is deciduous, *E. glutinosa (pinnatifolia).* It forms an upright, bushy shrub to about 15 ft. by 12 ft., well clothed to the ground, has pinnate leaves that turn to brilliant oranges and scarlets in autumn, and bears in August/September 2-inch white flowers with delicate buff anthers; the plant when grown well is smothered in flowers so much they hide the foliage. 'Flore Pleno' is a rarish form with double flowers. Both these eucryphias will grow on limestone soils, which their evergreen relatives will not, but they like a position with their roots in a cool, moist soil with plenty of peat and leaf-mold added, and their heads in the sun. Young specimens should be mulched to ensure a cool soil. Very lovely. Half-ripe cuttings; difficult. Tolerate light frost.

## Euonymus/Spindle tree

The charm of the deciduous members of this genus lies in their autumn coloring and in their colorful fruits. *E. alatus* has a ''winged,'' corky bark and foliage that in autumn has crimson and scarlet coloring, 7 ft. by 7 ft. '*E. europaeus* 'Atropurpureus' has purple leaves, and 'Aucubifolius' has leaves mottled yellow; both are more effective than the type.

## Exochorda/Pearl bush

*E. giraldii* and *E. grandiflora* are grown. Spectacular May-flowering white-flowered shrubs. 5 ft. by 8 ft. The long arching branches are covered with flowers each 2-in. across. Flowers are borne on the previous season's wood. Prune only to thin out weak growth. Any soil; sun. Half-ripe cuttings.

# Forsythia/Golden Bells

Among the brightest of spring flowering shrubs, renowned for their profusion of golden bell-shaped flowers. All are easy to grow in any fertile
soil, preferably in sun. The finest is *F.* × 'Lynwood', with very righ yellow flowers, 6 ft. by 6 ft. *F.* × 'Spring Glory', 8 ft. by 6 ft., has larger
flowers which smother the branches. *F. suspensa* is a rather rambling
pseudo-climber, ideal for using to cover a garden shed, flowers pale yellow. *F. viridissima* 'Bronxensis' is a useful dwarf to 3 ft. by 3 ft., bright
yellow flowers a little later than the others. Cut out flowering shoots as
soon as they have flowered. Half-ripe cuttings taken between July and
September, or hardwood cuttings taken October/December; layers.

# Fuschia

Among the most charming of late summer flowering shrubs for the
South, the fuschias are hardier than is generally realized. They behave
like herbaceous plants, the wood usually being killed to ground level in
winter. They flower from July until frost. Flower equally well in sun or
shade. Among the best are *F. gracilis,* a delicate little shrub with delicate
branches and slender flowers, red and purple. *F. magellanica* is similar
but larger flowered; *F. magellanica* 'Riccartonii' is one of the hardiest
with scarlet and purple flowers. 'Margaret' has very large flowers with
reflexed carmine sepals and a frilled petunia skirt; 'Mrs. Popple', also
very hardy, with a weeping habit, has large flowers, carmine with a clear
violet skirt; 'Tom Thumb' is a compact little dwarf with dainty flowers,
carmine and purple. If doubtful as to the hardiness of any fuschias you
plant, try some coarse mulch over them through the winter in mild climates. Increase by soft cuttings any time from July till frost.

# Genista

Another group of brooms; all have yellow flowers and are generally
longer lived than Cytisus. Their cultural requirements are the same. The
tallest is *G. aethnensis,* the Mount Etna broom, growing to 15 ft. by 10
ft., flowers June/July, and is a blaze of brilliant yellow — looking rather
like a golden fountain. *G. hispanica* is a complete contrast, reaching only
2 ft. but spreading widely in time, flowers bright yellow, June. Useful for
the front of the border. Both need full sun. Increase the first by seed, the
second by half-ripe cuttings.

Fuschias are good summer-flowering shrubs, having a remarkably long season — from July till first frost.

Golden bells or forsythia, one of the most spectacular of spring flowering shrubs. It does particularly well on poor soils.

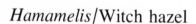

## *Hamamelis*/Witch hazel

The finest of all winter-flowering deciduous shrubs, with large hazel-like leaves which color well in autumn and curiously twisted, strap-shaped petals, usually yellow, red at the base, heavily scented, the flowers lasting for nearly two months. Slow-growing but ultimately tall — 10 ft. by 8 ft. *H. mollis* is probably the best, certainly most often planted; 'Jelena' has butter-yellow flowers suffused rich coppery red; 'Pallida' has extra strongly scented flowers of a paler sulphur yellow.

## *Hibiscus*

*H. syriacus,* shrub althea is among the most useful of late flowering shrubs, producing their 3-in. funnel-shaped blooms in August/September. 8 ft. by 4 ft. Very late starting into growth, often showing no

signs of life the first year after planting till June. 'Blue Bird' has large single blue flowers; 'Hamabo' blush pink flowers; 'Montrous Dorothy Crane' very large white flowers with a crimson center and 'Rubis Woodbridge' large carmine flowers. No routine pruning needed, though old specimens can be cut right back to old wood. Layering. *H. moscheutos* - Rose Mallow excellent for wet areas, flowers 5-6 in. diameter white, pink, red.

## *Hippophae*/Sea Buckthorn

One species, *H. rhamnoides,* is grown for its silvery, willow-like leaves and enormous crops of orange berries in autumn. 10 ft. by 10 ft. Plant one male for every three females; cross pollination is needed to achieve fruiting. Full sun. Half-ripe cutting.

## *Hoheria*/New Zealand ribbon woods

Beautiful shrubs producing such large quantities of almost translucent white flowers in July/August that they bow the branches down. Slightly tender and useful in mild, humid frost-free climates. Any soil, good on limestone. 10 ft. to 8 ft. No pruning. Half-ripe cuttings.

## *Hydrangea*/Florist hydrangea

Valuable because they produce their spectacular heads of red, pink, blue or white flowers in late summer, from July onwards, the heads lasting in color till the frosts. Good on any soil, but gross feeders. *H. macrophylla* is not completely hardy, especially the flower buds. They flower on the tips of the previous season's growth, and if this gets cut by frost there will be no flowers. The only routine pruning needed is to remove weak growth, old gnarled unproductive wood and the old flower heads: these operations should be carried out in early April. Most people believe that hydrangeas turn blue on acid soils, but stay pink on alkaline soils. In fact life is not quite that simple. Many pink varieties will never turn blue, no matter how acid your soil. On alkaline soils hydrangeas that will blue can be blued by digging in alum powder around the roots in spring: conversely, blue hydrangeas can be turned pink on acid soils by digging in ground limestone. There are two basic flower types: *Hortensias,* with large rounded heads composed entirely of large, sterile flowers; and *Lacecaps* which have pyramidal heads in which not all the flowers are of the large, sterile type. Among the best are:

**Hortensias**

DEEP BLUE Marechal Foch, Parsifal and Goliath.

DEEP PINK Altona, Europa and Hamburg.

RED Hatfield Rose, Westfalen and Ami Pasquier. The reds are all smaller growing than the others — 2 ft. to 3 ft. instead of 4 ft. to 5 ft.

WHITE Mme. E. Mouilliere.

**Lacecaps** Blue Bird — to 3 ft. — blues well. Lanarth, pure white. Bluewave, very vigorous, late flowering, needs help to blue well. One other hydrangea is well worth growing and that is *H. paniculata* which carries huge conical heads of sterile white flowers. The variety 'Grandiflora' has even larger heads. The plant is hardy, and flower heads 18 in. long can be produced by cutting it down to the ground each spring and feeding it liberally. Soft cuttings from non-flowering shoots.

## *Hypericum*/St. John's Wort

Grown for their large rich yellow flowers produced from June till October, they will grow in any soil in full sun. The best are *H. patulum,* 4 ft. by 3 ft., the leaves turning rich crimson in autumn and followed by bright red seed heads, and the variety 'Hidcote' which is similar but has even larger flowers. *H. × moserianum* has large yellow flowers with red stamens very freely borne, and makes excellent ground cover. The variety 'Tricolor' has leaves variegated pink, cream and green. Half-ripe cuttings or offshoots.

## *Kerria*

*K. japonica* is a popular and easily grown shrub with green, suckering stems and rather yellow flowers. The form usually grown is double, but the single form is just as good. Dislikes full sun, and will grow in heavy, even wet soils. Prune out flowering shoots after flowering. Slightly tender on exposed sites. Suckers.

## *Kolkwitzia*/Beauty bush

One species only is grown, *K. amabilis,* which has a graceful arching habit of growth, produces masses of small pink tubular flowers in May/June. Any soil, full sun. Cut out old shoots after flowering. Half-ripe cuttings.

## Lilac: see *Syringa*

Witch hazels are treasured both for their scented yellow
flowers produced in the dead of winter and for their
autumn color. The one shown here is *Hamamelis mollis*.

Hydrangeas are probably the most universally planted of
summer flowering shrubs. The showy flowers are sterile
and remain on the plant, gradually fading, for months.

The beauty bush *Kolkwitzia amabilis* is similar to the better
known weigela but far more graceful in growth and far
more floriferous.

# Magnolia

Among the most opulent of all woody plants, most are too large-growing for small gardens. By far the most suitable is *M. stellata,* the star magnolia, which produces enormous numbers of 3-in. pure white flowers in March, slow growing to about 8 ft. by 5 ft.; 'Rosea' has pinkish flowers, and 'Rubra' rather wine-colored pink flowers and a weak constitution. *M. lilflora nigra* produces its flowers with the leaves during April/May and sporadically throughout the rest of the summer. The flowers are tulip-shaped, a rich purple. *M. × soulangeana* is the most commonly seen magnolia, producing beautiful chalice shaped blooms before the leaves in March/April. It will ultimately make a spreading bush 20 ft. by 20 ft. The variety 'Stricta' has a columnar habit and is the best for general planting. *M. sieboldii,* to 30 ft., is quite different producing its pure white flowers with a red cluster of anthers in the center, cup shaped and downwards pointing, in mid-summer; *M. wilsonii* is similar. Both produce curious cerise fruit cones. Enrich the soil with peat or leaf-mold for magnolias, and never dig anywhere near their roots, it will kill them. Increase the last two by seed, the others by layering.

# *Paeonia*/Tree peonies

No other shrubs can match these for the sheer size and brilliance of coloring of the flowers, which are like huge poppies, as much as 18 in. across, single, semi-double or double, red, pink, white or bi-colored. There are over 5,000 named varieties of *P. suffruticosa,* but they are difficult to propagate, and one has to buy what is available. Plant in a position sheltered from early morning sun, with the graft 3 in. below the soil. In autumn, cut back any improperly ripened wood to large buds on well-ripened wood. *P. × lemoinei* is the name given to a race of mainly yellow-flowered hybrids. Among the best are: 'L' Esperance', bright yellow; 'La Lorraine', huge rich yellow double, 'Alice Harding', enormous sulphur yellow and 'Souvenire de Maxim Cornu', coppery orange with yellow lights. Flowers are large, heavy and may need support to hold flowers upright. All are slow-growing to about 5 ft. by 5 ft. They have beautifully divided leaves, often pink or copper in spring, and often with a silvery bloom on them through summer. Plants are usually grafted on stock of herbaceous peonies. Increase by seed, stratified and left out of doors until germinated, then potted up individually.

## *Perovskia*/Russian sage

Neither Russian nor a sage, none the less an attractive late-flowering shrub. The finest is × 'Blue Spire', the whole plant being covered in silvery-white down, except the bright blue terminal flower spikes, borne in late summer. 4 ft. by 3 ft. Likes a hot sunny place and preferably sandy soil. Prune back hard to the base of the previous season's growth each April. Soft cuttings in May. Useful only in frost free areas.

## *Philadelphus*/Mock orange

Eternally popular shrubs with fragrant white flowers, excellent for flower arranging. All will grow easily in any soil, preferably in sun, and all flower June/July. Among the best are 'Beauclerk', 6 ft. by 6 ft., very large sweetly scented white flowers; 'Belle Etoile', 6 ft. by 5 ft., exquisitely scented very large white flowers with a slight pink flush at the base of the petals; and 'Manteau d'Hermine', 3 ft. by 4 ft., exceptionally free-flowering with double creamy white vanilla-scented flowers. Prune out shoots that have flowered immediately after flowering. Half-ripe cuttings in July/August, hardwood cuttings November/December.

## *Potentilla*

The shrubby potentillas are all forms of *P. fruticosa,* and have yellow, white or, rarely, reddish flowers like rather small single roses. Perhaps their greatest virtue is the length of their flowering season — from May until November. Among the best are 'Tangerine', orange; 'Longacre', large pale yellow; 'Primrose Beauty', deep cream flowers and greyish leaves and 'Sunset' with flowers varying from deep orange to brick red. All have trifoliate leaves, grow to about 4 ft., need no pruning, do best in sunny situations and are easily increased by layering half-ripe cuttings.

## *Poncirus*/Hardy orange

A fascinating plant that has been known variously as *Aegle sepiaria, Citrus trifoliata* and now finally as *Poncirus trifoliata,* it really is related to the orange and bears large white scented flowers which are followed by small, bitter oranges. 8 ft. by 6 ft. The stout branches are armed with fearsome 2-in. thorns, and the twigs are green. Sun; no pruning. Seed; half-ripe cuttings. Tolerates cold to 25°F.

Magnolias are probably the most exotic-looking of all shrubs. They are not nearly as difficult to grow as many people think. The one shown here is the popular *Magnolis* × *soulangeana*.

The potentillas are all easily grown shrubs of neat, compact habit with a very long flowering season.

Tree peonies *Paeonia suffruticosa* have the largest flowers of any hardy shrub. Colors range from white through cream to yellow as well as pink, red and purple. Many also have interesting foliage with a blue or pinkish bloom.

## Prunus

A huge family which includes the flowering cherries as well as the peaches, almonds, nectarines and the cherry laurel. Only two members are truly shrubby. *P. tenella* is a dwarf, suckering shrub from Siberia, as hardy as they come, growing to about 4 ft. but spreading slowly and indefinitely, covered in spring in gay pink blossoms. The form 'Fire Hill' has bright red flowers. Cut out about half the old flowering shoots directly after flowering. Increase by division. The other is really a peach, *P. triloba,* always grown in its double form 'Flore Pleno'. Every twig of the previous season's growth is covered in icing-pink double rosette-like flowers in April. Prune hard after flowering. 4 ft. by 5 ft. Usually sold as grafted plants — watch for suckers! Increase by layering.

## Rhus/Sumac

(See also *Cotinus*.) Rather tree-like shrubs with pinnate leaves (like those of an ash tree, but larger), grown mainly for their autumn coloring. This is best when the plants are grown in full sun on very poor soil, and the leaves turn every possible hue of yellow, pink, orange and scarlet. The branches are very thick, somewhat hairy, and the plant takes on a rather ugly outline in winter when bare. 12 ft. by 15 ft. The best species is *R. typhina,* the so-called stag's horn sumac, with leaves up to 2 ft. long. The variety 'Laciniata' has very finely cut leaves and is even better. Suckers.

## Ribes/Flowering currants

Very popular and easily grown shrubs, 10 ft. by 8 ft., thriving in any soil, in sun or some shade. They produce hanging clusters of pink flowers in April. Usually grown is *R. sanguineum,* which has rather washed-out pink flowers: much better colored, being deeper and purer pink, is 'King Edward VII'. Prune hard after flowering only to maintain a desired shape. Layer. *R. alpinum* is useful for shady sites.

## Romneya/California tree poppy

One of the most lovely of all deciduous shrubs, with purest white 6-in. poppy-like flowers borne July till September: the flowers have a huge center boss of fluffy golden anthers. Tends to behave like a herbaceous perennial in colder areas. Native to California and Mexico. 5 ft. by 6 ft. Leaves poppy-like but smooth and grey-green. Two species are grown, *R. coutleri* and *R. trichocalyx.* Hybrids between the two, known as *R.* ×

*hybrida* are also excellent. Full sun, any soil. Cut back almost to ground level each April. Suckers; root cuttings. Hates root disturbance.

# *Rosa*/Roses

All the roses normally grown in gardens, the floribundas and the hybrid teas, will grow just as well in the shrub border as they will in beds solely devoted to them. Certainly they will suffer far less from the pests and diseases which are such a problem when they are all grown together in one bed. The mere fact that they are planted with other shrubs between them will stop any pest or disease that settles on one from moving to the next one with quite the same speed as they do when all together in one bed. Curiously enough, most of them will look more effective when grown in this way: the sheer size of their flowers will be far more noticeable when grown this way, than it is when they are grown all together, a whole bed of roses all with large flowers. And they are well worth including in the shrub border. Indeed, it would not be complete without them. There are no other shrubs that have such a long flowering season, or quite such perfectly shaped flowers. Moreover, when planted in the shrub border they can be placed so that smaller shrubs hide the bare stems at ground level. The smaller sorts can be planted nearer the front of the border, taller-growing kinds farther back. The choice of roses is so wide that one really can only select the best according to one's own personal ideas of what constitutes a good rose, but it is worth remembering that the paler colors look best from a distance: white, pale yellow and pale pink are all good even from a distance. The darker colors, especially the really dark reds, are definitely not good from a distance: they just don't show up. For varieties, consult specialist growers or their catalogues.

In addition to the roses normally grown in gardens there are over 500 species of rose, usually known as 'shrub roses'. These in the main have a shorter season than the more common roses, tending to produce all their flowers in one magnificent flush, but on the other hand need no pruning. Most also have large, colorful fruits in late autumn. Among the best for general planting are *Rosa californica* 'Plena', 6 ft. by 6 ft., deep rich pink semi-double fragrant flowers in mid-summer, fern-like leaves, small red hips; *R. farreri* 'Persetosa', with almost hair-like thorns and masses of single pink flowers in May/June followed by tiny but very bright red hips, 7 ft. by 6 ft.; *R. multibracteata* 'Cerise Bouquet', 4 ft. by 5 ft., very large double Tyrian rose-purple flowers, remarkably free-flowering, with a graceful, semi-weeping habit; *R. virginiana*, 6 ft. spreading slowly, pink leaves in spring, deep pink flowers in mid-summer, good autumn color and masses of bright red hips, very hardy. Seed, layers, suckers.

Roses, though often considered in a class of their own, are among the most spectacular of all shrubs and can be used like any other shrub.

## *Spartium*/Spanish broom

See also *Genista* and *Cytisus*. Only one is really good, *S. junceum,* with hollow rush-like stems bearing at their tips huge spikes of large pea-type flowers, deep yellow and wonderfully scented. 7 ft. by 6 ft. Full sun, good on poor soils. Short-lived. Seed or half-ripe cuttings.

## *Spiraea*

A very free-flowering, easily grown group of shrubs. The individual flowers are small, but borne in dense clusters which makes them effective. The earliest to flower is *S. thunbergii,* 4 ft. by 5 ft., a twiggy mass of white flowers in March/April. This is followed by *S. arguta* (Bridal Wreath), 6 ft. by 6 ft., covered in showers of white flowers all along the branches of the previous season's growth in April/May. The largest of all is *S. vanhoutei,* 10 ft. by 7 ft., again with masses of white flowers in May. Of the later flowering spireas the best are forms of *S. japonica,* the finest being 'Anthony Waterer', with flat heads of rich crimson flowers in July/August, 3 ft. by 3 ft. Division and softwood cuttings.

## *Symplocos*/Sweetleaf

Only one species, *S. paniculata (cratagoides),* is grown. Rare but worth while. Slow growing to 10 ft. by 5 ft. Leaves small, bright green in spring, clusters of white, hawthorn-like slightly scented flowers, yellow autumn color and brilliant turquoise berries remaining on the branches through winter. Plant two or more to obtain seed. Fruits best in a sheltered position facing south or west. Seed.

## *Syringa*/Lilac

Too well known to need much description, lilacs are treasured for their large pyramidal flowers as well as for their scent. What is not generally appreciated is that they are gross feeders for water and plant food and are not, therefore, the best of companions in a mixed shrub border. Most tend to sucker, some faster than others; digging the soil around the roots increases the rate and amount of suckering. Suckers should be removed with a sharp, upward pull. Lilacs are also large-growing, ultimately reaching 15 ft. by 15 ft. There are so many to choose from, but the following are among the best:

**Single** 'Charles X', long, purple-red flowers, has been popular a very long time; 'Etna', deep claret-purple fading to lilac, later flowering than most; 'Madame Francisque Morel', enormous flower heads of mauve-pink, large individual 'pips'; 'Maud Notcutt', huge flower spikes of pure white; 'Mont Blanc', long, pure white flower spikes, with a touch of green that seems to make the flowers even whiter; 'Souvenire de Louis Spaeth', wine red, probably the most popular of all lilacs, very reliable. **Double** 'Charles Joly', deep purplish-red, late flowering; 'Michel Buchner', pale rosy-lilac, huge dense panicles, few suckers; 'Princess Clementine', creamy yellow in bud opening pure white, very free flowering. To get the best out of lilacs every flower truss should be removed after flowering. This can be quite a chore on a large plant, but it is well worth while, you will get nearly twice as much flower the following year. It also pays to fertilize lilacs. This should not be placed right up against the plant, but in a ring where the branches end — for that is where the feeding roots will be. Suckers; half-ripe cuttings.


## *Tamarix*/Tamarisk

Grown for their feather appearance and for their soft green spring foliage and yellow autumn leaves, rather than for their flowers, which are a bit ineffective. Never shapely, they form leggy, rambly shrubs up to 10 ft. by 8 ft. Less tall and less leggy if cut annually almost to ground level. *T. tetrandra* and *T. parviflora* flower in May/June on the previous season's wood. Rather more showy are *T. pentandra* and its forms, notably 'Pink Cascade' and 'Rubra' which flower in July-September on the current season's growth. Excellent by the sea, where they will grow in almost pure sand. Inland they need full sun and good soil. Hardwood cuttings.

# Viburnum

A large genus of both deciduous and evergreen shrubs. They are so variable that anyone gardening on a limestone soil would do well to consider using them in quantity and in variety. *V. farreri* (formerly and probably better known as *V. fragrans*) is the most widely planted. Its great virtue is that it produces its pinkish, strongly almond-scented flowers early, in April: its great failing is that it forms a rambling great tangle of wood 10 ft. tall spreading almost indefinitely by suckers and layering itself wherever a branch touches the ground. A dwarf form, *V. farreri* 'Compacta' to 3 ft., is more desirable, forming a dense, twiggy little bush; needs a hot site and sandy soil to flower freely. *V. bodnantense* 'Dawn' suckers less, has rich pink flowers. *V. carlesii* is a fine spring flowering species (April/May), with pink buds opening to pure white and a good scent: 5 ft. by 6 ft. *V. carlcephalum* has larger flowers in huge bunches, but grows ultimately to 10 ft. by 8 ft. *V. burkwoodii* is similar, also growing to 10 ft. by 8 ft., but has polished leaves which color well before falling. *V. opulus*, the guelder rose, somewhat resembles a hydrangea, with an outer ring of large sterile flowers and an inner ring of small, fertile flowers. The finest form is *V. opulus* 'Sterile' in which all the flowers are sterile — forming a large ball-shaped flower-head — giving it the popular name snowball tree. 12 ft. by 15 ft. The dwarf from *V. opulus* 'Compactum' grows to only 5 ft. by 15 ft. Both have good autumn color, and both the type plant and 'Compactum' have bright red berries in autumn. Another snowball tree, *V. tomentosum plicatum* is better for smaller gardens; 6 ft. by 8 ft. Large snowball type flowers on gracefully arching branches. Layer; half-ripe cuttings.

# Weigela

Popular easily-grown shrubs with masses of inch-long trumpet-shaped flowers in various shades. Any soil, sun or little shade. Flowers are borne all along wood of the previous season's growth, and flowering shoots should be cut out after flowering. Dull leaves and little charm of habit. *W. florida* 'Variegata' is an exception, with bright golden variegated foliage and masses of rose pink flowers. The others are all forms of *W. × hybrida*. Some of the best are 'Newport Red', brightest red flowers of the genus, 'Bristol Ruby', ruby red, 'Conquete', rose pink and 'Abel Carriere', rose red with a yellow throat. All reach about 6 ft. by 6 ft. Half-ripe or hardwood cuttings.

The viburnums are a huge genus of deciduous and evergreen species, some grown for their flowers, some for their leaves, and some, like this one, for their colorful berries.

Lilacs are deservedly among the most popular of all shrubs, both for their large flower heads and their unique scent. They are however, greedy feeders and little else will grow near them.

# 8 Evergreen Shrubs

Evergreens differ from deciduous shrubs in more ways than simply the obvious one of retaining their leaves through winter. In the first place there are probably more sumptuous flowers to be found among the evergreens than there are among the deciduous shrubs, and in the second place they provide a year-round screen for the garden. But they do have their disadvantages. They nearly all come from warmer climates, so they are not so well adapted to the cold winters of the northern states as the deciduous shrubs and some of them tend to look a bit "worn" by the end of winter. The other factor that should always be borne in mind when planting them is that most of them also come from a rather damp climate, and usually from one with a higher atmospheric humidity than is found in this country. In general, this is why most of the finest specimens of evergreen shrubs are to be found in the warmer, wetter parts of the United States: it is also why a great many of them are grown in woodland conditions, since the atmospheric humidity in woodland is invariably substantially higher than in the open. All this should not, however, discourage anyone from trying evergreens if they want to. There are quite a number that are hardy to southern New England — like the Japanese holly *Ilex crenata* and its varieties. All evergreens do best if planted in a soil that has been enriched with peat or leaf-mold which helps to retain moisture better than ordinary soil. Some of the others come from hot sunny climates, and are best grown in sandy soil at the foot of a south or west wall.

As for effectiveness, generally speaking those with glossy leaves look less drab in winter than those with matt leaves. Variegated evergreens really come into their own in winter, and again it is those with glossy leaves that look the best.

In general very few evergreens need pruning: most of them simply need dead-heading. Any pruning should be done right after flowering. Many will only grow on acid soil, and where this is the case it is invariably mentioned in the descriptive list that follows.

# Abelia

Beautiful shrubs with small leaves and tubular flowers: not spectacular, but they have a quiet charm. One species is hardy, *A. grandiflora,* 4 ft. by 4 ft., flowers palest pink, almost white, ½-in. long, July till frost. Prune out old branches periodically. Half-ripe cuttings.

# Berberis/Barberries

(See also Deciduous Shrubs.) The evergreen types are, in the main, fully hardy, will grow in any soil, sun or part shade, are no trouble, need no pruning and keep the weeds down. On the other hand none is wildly exciting. Among the best are *B. darwinii,* probably best of all, 8 ft. by 4 ft., tiny, prickly dark green leaves, brilliant orange-red flowers April/May, bluish-purple berries in autumn. Seeds freely. *B.* × *stenophylla,* 10 ft. by 6 ft., arching branches covered in bright yellow flowers, April/May, followed by pink berries; quickly forms a dense thicket. The variety 'Corallina Compacta' is useful for the front of the border, growing 1 ft. by 2 ft., with rich golden flowers. *B. verruculosa,* 4 ft. by 4 ft., arching branches wreathed in very thickly set dark green leaves, white beneath, clusters of drooping golden-yellow flowers May, followed by black fruits covered with a blue bloom in autumn: some of the foliage turns crimson in autumn — unusual among evergreens. *B. buxifolia* 'Nana' is another dwarf, 2 ft. by 2 ft., yellow flowers in April and purplish winter foliage; prickle-free. All generally hardy to southern New England. Half-ripe cuttings are slow to root; layers or suckers are generally the easiest means of increase; seed is also easy but the barberries hybridize readily.

# Camellia

Strictly for acid soils, camellias are among the most glamorous of all shrubs: they have a quality and dignity about them that no other genus can rival. Anyone with an alkaline soil can grow them in tubs in a lime-free soil: the soil should be dressed with flowers of sulphur to keep it acid. Well adapted to the South and the Pacific Northwest, and other areas of mild winters. They should always be planted in a situation where they are sheltered from the early morning sun: it is not frost that destroys their flower buds, but rapid thawing. If planted out of reach of early morning sun the thawing will be gradual and will do less damage; the north or west side of a shrub or building is ideal. Essentially forest undershrubs, camellias must have some shade during part of the day: too much sun scorches the foliage — too much shade and they will not flower freely. They need more sun in the north of the country than in the south. Most of those mentioned here are fully hardy. Camellias are especially satisfactory in the southeastern states north to Virginia and Maryland and in Washington, Oregon and California. Slow-growing, they ultimately form very large plants, to 15 ft. by 12 ft.. They transplant well, and even specimens 8 or 10 ft. tall recover quickly after a move. The sorts usually grown are cultivars of *Camellia japonica,* which has dark green glossy leaves. The flowers can be single, semi-double or fully double, and vary considerably in form. Colors range from white through pinks to scarlet and crimson, with bi-colors as well. There are over 5,000 named cultivars, but the naming is somewhat confused. In general few garden centers carry more than a dozen or fifteen varieties, but these are usually among the most popular. The following are excellent kinds but may not be hardy in the more northern areas. Check with other gardeners for hardy cultivars in your area. Pure whites are generally easily browned by frosts. Some of the best are 'Countessa Lavinia Maggi', white striped and splashed crimson, pointed petals; occasionally sports pure pink flowers. 'Adolphe Audusson', semi-double bright scarlet with a large boss of yellow stamens. 'Mars' is very similar. 'Jupiter', large trumpet-shaped single of bright scarlet with a good center. 'Mrs. D. W. Davies', huge cup-shaped flowers of pale blush pink with a broad mass of center stamens: has tremendous quality. 'Drama Girl', slightly more tender than most and best against a west wall, has the largest flowers of all hardy camellias, up to 9 in. across, brightest carmine. 'Lady Clare', one of the best pinks, with a graceful weeping habit, very large flowers: 'Furoan', medium-sized pink flowers with a good center; very pleasing. 'Betty Sheffield Supreme', large flowers, white with a pink picottee edge; superb. 'Elegans', formal semi-double pink, probably the most widely planted of all camellias. 'Donkelarii', very large semi-double with white streaks. 'Grand Slam', huge double deep red. *C. saluenensis* is a smaller growing species with matt, net-veined leaves a pure pink trumpet-shaped about 4 in. across. Very lovely but less well known; detests cold winds, though withstands frost well. This has been crossed with *C. japonica* to produce a hybrid known as *C. × williamsii,* the best of which is 'Donation' — probably one of the finest camellia ever raised: tall, narrow habit, small, matt leaves and large semi-double flowers of a vibrant yet soft pink shot with darker veins; very spectacular; flowers when very small. 'Salutation', 'Inspiration' and 'Parkside' are other good forms of this race. All flower from January till May, depending on the weather. No pruning needed. Half-ripe cuttings to July; layers; seed is always worth growing on, but needs heat to germinate: the hard seed cases should be nicked.

Camellias have flowers that look as though they were made of wax — of tremendous weight and substance. Although the picture shows a camellia being grown under glass, nearly all are perfectly hardy in the South. Acid soil is essential.

## *Ceanothus*/Californian lilacs

(See also Deciduous Shrubs.) The finest ceanothus, those with the purest and brightest blue flowers, all belong here. They are all rather more tender than the deciduous species, and are best grown against a sunny wall. The flowers are individually tiny, borne in dense spikes produced in great quantities. They should be planted very young from pots, and never moved once planted. Any soil. Plant in spring. Most satisfactory along the Pacific Coast. *C. prostratus* has a weeping, creeping habit and forming a large, low mound about 2 ft. by 8 ft.; it is much hardier than the other evergreen species, makes good ground cover and has sky blue flowers. *C. thrysiflorus,* a native of the west coast, flowers in March with blue flowers. Half-ripe cuttings in September.

# Choisya/Mexican orange

One species, *C. ternata*, 6 ft. by 8 ft., needs a position sheltered by other shrubs or by a wall, is best with a little shade since full sun makes the leaves yellow, and will grow in any soil. Very choice. Leaves bright polished mid-green, darker in shade, lighter in sun, very aromatic when crushed, masses of waxy white starry flowers May and then sporadically through the year. In areas with mild winters. No routine pruning. Good for cuttings, but cut to keep shapely. Layers; half-ripe cuttings, July.

# Cistus

Sometimes known as rock roses, a name also used for Helianthemum (q.v.). Delightful shrubs with pointed, leathery leaves which give off a pungent aroma in damp weather and large, disc-like flowers, usually white or pink, often with good markings in the center, opening in great numbers each day but fading again by late afternoon, flowering through mid-summer. Any soil, but especially useful on poor soils. Full sun. In cold districts best against a wall, best where temperature does not go below 20°F. None is very long-lived — 10 years or so, and none is very hardy. Among the best are *C.* × *hybridius*, 5 ft. by 5 ft., rosy-pink buds, white flowers with a yellow flush; one of the hardiest; red stems. *C.* × *cyprius*, 6 ft. by 4 ft., 3-in. white flowers with a maroon blotch at the base of the petals. Sage green leaves. *C.* × *purpureus*, 4 ft. by 4 ft., very large flowers, purple-red with deep black-red blotches. *C. crispus*, 4 ft. by 4 ft., deep rose pink flowers from June till October. *C.* × *loretii*, 2 ft. by 3 ft., white flowers with a crimson blotch to the petals. Does best on good soil. No pruning. Half-ripe cuttings, July.

# Cotoneaster

(See also Deciduous Shrubs.) The evergreen species embrace a range of plants from prostrate spreaders to small trees. Flowers often pass unnoticed, but the berries are usually conspicuous: they are also liked by birds. The lowest growing is *C. dammeri*, 4 in. spreading indefinitely, fully weed-proof, rooting as it grows, glossy leaves good white flowers, June, very large cerise berries. *C. microphyllus* has tiny, glossy leaves and a mounding habit, 3 ft. but spreading, the branch ends rooting; white flowers May; pinkish-red berries. Of the taller growing species *C. franchetii* is probably the best, 10 ft. by 10 ft., grey-green oval leaves, and small orange-red berries in great quantities. Seedlings may not come true to type; half-ripe cuttings, July/August; easy.

## *Cortaderia*/Pampas Grass

Not strictly woody, but such a permanent plant and so large-growing that it fits in well in the shrub border. Long, narrow grass-like leaves in great tufts and huge feathery plumes in autumn. Any soil. Sun. Burn off dead foliage in spring. *C. selloana,* 5 ft., silvery plumes August-October. *C. pumila,* a dwarf form by 4 ft. *C.* 'Sunningdale Silver', 6 ft., a superb form with loose silky spikes. Division.

## *Desfontainea*/Chilean holly

One species, *D. spinosa,* a tender evergreen with small, holly-like leaves and 2-in. tubular yellow flowers, tipped orange, borne from July till September. Very slow growing but ultimately 6 ft. by 5 ft. Acid soil, plenty of peat or leaf-mold mixed in. Flowers best in a cool position in shade. Seed; half-ripe cuttings; layers.

## *Elaeagnus*

*E. pungens maculata* ('Aureo-maculata'), is one of the brightest of all variegated shrubs. Leaves oval, pointed, the center bright daffodil gold, surrounded by a lighter yellow, streaks of pale green and a dark green margin. Really comes into its own in the winter sunshine. Flowers insignificant but strongly scented. November. Suitable for mild climates only. Any soil; sun. Cut out any green-leaved shoots. 10 ft. by 10 ft. but slow growing. Half-ripe cuttings. August/September; slow to root.

## *Embothrium*/Chilean fire bush

Probably the most brilliantly colored of all flowering shrubs that can be grown out of doors in mild climates, an established plant is breath-taking. Generally regarded as tender, one form is hardy in southern California and similar climates. Flower tubular, 2 in. long, like individual pips of honeysuckle, produced in clusters all around and all along the young branches, being borne in such quantities that they literally hide the branch, brightest orange-scarlet. Plant very young from pots in acid soil with plenty of peat and/or leaf-mold mixed in. Pinch out growing tip to keep bushy: never prune. Ultimately 20 ft. tall, but narrow in habit. Tends to sucker slowly: these should be carefully removed for increase. *Never* disturb the roots; plant ground cover around it when newly planted and let this keep the weeds down.

# *Erica:* see Heathers

## *Escallonia*

Quick-growing summer and early autumn semi-evergreen shrubs with small flowers borne in huge quantities. Leaves very dark, glossy, small. Any soil; sun. Do very well near the sea; need the shelter of a wall or other shrubs in cold districts. Among the best are 'C. F. Ball', 8 ft. by 5 ft., large deep red flowers; 'Peach Blossom', 6 ft. by 5 ft., good pink flowers; 'Slieve Donard', 8 ft. by 5 ft., apple-blossom pink flowers, very fine; *E.* × *iveyi,* 8 ft. by 6 ft., white flowers. No pruning; half-ripe cuttings, July or layers.

## *Eucryphia*

(See also Deciduous Shrubs.) The evergreen eucryphias all need an acid soil with plenty of peat and/or leaf-mold added, are rather tender when young but quite hardy once established and so spectacular that they should be tried wherever conditions suit. The best is *E.* × *nymansensis* 'Nymansay', which forms a narrow column 15 ft. to 20 ft. tall but seldom more than 4 ft. or 5 ft. wide and bears in August 2½-in. white flowers with pink anthers that smother the whole plant; fragrant. Not fast growing. Roots should be shaded with stones when young, and with ground-cover plants when established. Flowers best in sun; prefers shelter of other trees from cold winds for mild climates of the south. Layers; half-ripe cuttings — rather slow to root.

## *Euonymus*/Wintercreeper

(See also Deciduous Shrubs.) One evergreen member, *E. fortunei gracilis variegatus* forms a good ground-cover subject in sun or shade — even quite deep shade. It will also run up the side of building to 20 ft. Normally grows 15 in. and spreads slowly. Green and white variegated leaves, tinted pink in winter. Seldom flowers, flowers insignificant. Division.

Pampas grass *Cortaderia* 'Argentea' is one of the joys of the garden in late summer and autumn. A little known trick is to burn off the dead leaves. This keeps the plants much tidier.

# *Euphorbia*/Spurge

Strictly for those who want something out of the ordinary, the spurges are grown mainly for their architectural effect. Thick fleshy stems and grey-green spoon shaped leaves, producing in spring great terminal cylindrical masses of yellowish-green bracts — April-June. Can be rather sprawling: cut old wood after flowering periodically but not frequently. The finest is *E. characias*. It reaches about 4 ft. by 4 ft., any soil, full sun, best in the shelter of a wall or other shrubs. Seed; half-ripe cuttings. The milky sap can irritate the skin and cause temporary blindness if rubbed against the eyes. Belongs to the same genus as the poinsettia.

# *Fatsia*

*F. japonica* — foliage shrub with huge, 9-in. maple-like glossy ever-green leaves and thick stems. Any soil. Tolerates light frost. Leaves look best in shade when they turn a very dark green; lighter green in sun. Flowers white in curious ball-shaped clusters in November followed by black fruits. About 8 ft. by 8 ft. — slow-growing. Seed; cuttings of firm wood.

# × *Fatshedera lizei*

An intergeneric hybrid between *Fatsia japonica* and English ivy. Forms a sprawling shrub about 3 ft. but spreading indefinitely with fine, maple-like leaves of a gay, glossy green, making excellent ground cover for shade. Looks lovely with *Tropaeolum speciosum* growing through it. Layers.

# *Garrya*/Silk Tassel bush

Remarkable Californian evergreen with dull grey-green leaves grown for its pale greyish catkins produced in February. Fast growing to 10 ft. by 8 ft. Best as a wall-shrub on any aspect, if grown in the open needs the shelter of other shrubs. Best in frost free areas. Male plants have better catkins than female plants, normally 6 in. long. The form 'James Roof' has catkins 18 in. long, but is more tender. Any soil. No routine pruning. Half-ripe cuttings, July-September; layers. Plant from pots and do not transplant.

# Halimium

Closely related to *Cistus* but with usually yellow flowers. Likes a hot, dry position in full sun. Moderately hardy, but likely to be lost in a severe winter. 3 ft. by 3 ft. Usually grown is *H. lasianthum* with small grey leaves and 1½-in. bright yellow flowers with a maroon blotch at the base of each petal. Half-ripe cuttings, July.

# Heathers

These are grouped together here for convenience, though botanically they belong to three genera, *Erica, Calluna* and *Daboecia*. They are in the main low-growing, acid-loving plants — though there are one or two taller species and some will grow on lime (see below). They make superb ground-cover plants, absolutely weed-proof, and most simply need a clip over with garden shears after flowering to keep them tidy. They look good at the front of the border, or when grown on their own in island beds, mixed with a few dwarf conifers. They flower best in full sun, and many also color in winter if fully exposed to frost. Dig in plenty of peat or leaf-mold before planting; plant close to good ground cover; make sure the ground is completely weed-free before planting.

**Heathers for lime** Only four species of heather will grow on lime soils, these are *Erica carnea* and its varieties, *E. mediterranea, E. darleyensis* and *E. terminalis*.

**Winter/Spring flowering heathers** *Erica carnea,* 12 in., flowers January-April; the type has deep pink flowers. 'Aurea' has golden foliage and deep pink flowers; 'December Red' is deep wine purple; 'King George', carmine flowers with brown tips; 'Springwood White', the best white, with showy chocolate-brown anthers; 'Springwood Pink', similar but rose-pink; 'Vivellii' is the deepest red heather, leaves turning dark bronze in winter. *E. mediterranea* is taller growing to 4 ft., gets cut back in hard winters but normally recovers, flowers smaller, pink, March-May. The above two have been crossed to produce *E.* × *darleyensis,* 2 ft.; 'A. T. Johnson', free-flowering deep magenta, December-April; 'J. H. Brummage', pink flowers, golden yellow foliage; 'Silver Beads', white flowers.

**Summer/Autumn flowering heathers** *Daboecia,* flowers in mild climates, closely related to *Erica,* 2½ ft., similar flowers but in drooping clusters, June-November. *D. cantabrica* 'Alba' has white flowers; 'Atropurpurea', deep pink flowers. *D. cinerea* 'Golden Drop' is grown for its coppery-golden foliage which turns rusty red in winter, seldom flowers, but very effective. *D. tetralix,* the native cross-leaved heath; 'Con Underwood' is the best form, grey-green mounds with crimson flowers.

The eucryphias have no common name, yet are among the most floriferous of all evergreens. The one shown here is *Eucryphia milliganii*.

*D. vulgaris,* the common native heath, also known as Scottish heather or Ling; 'Alba Plena' has double white flowers; 'County Wicklow', double pink flowers; 'Golden Haze', foliage purest gold all the year, flowers white; 'Goldsworth Crimson', deep crimson purple flowers; 'H. E. Beale', still one of the best, double pink flowers. *D. terminalis,* 5 ft. by 4 ft., pink flowers June-September, flowers turn russet and look good all winter, does best on lime. Mound-layering is the easiest means of increase, just hump sandy soil over the crown of the plant, it will root into this, lift and divide in autumn. Half-ripe cuttings; seed.

## *Hebe*/Veronica

A variable genus, some good in flower, mostly rather tender and best on the Pacific Coast or as a cool greenhouse plant, some resembling conifers and some making good ground cover.

**For Flower** These are mainly tender. Take a sprig each autumn and root it in a glass of water; if the plant is killed the cutting will quickly replace it. Flowers in terminal spikes. Among the best are 'Autumn Glory', small, purplish leaves, purple flowers, blooms most of the summer and autumn; 'Great Orme', 6-in. spikes of deep pink flowers, narrow, willow-like leaves; 'Andersonii Variegata', cream and pale green leaves, very effective, deep lavender flowers; 'Simon deleaux', carmine flowers. All grow about 4 ft. by 4 ft.

**Conifer-like** *H. cupressoides,* 4 ft. by 3 ft., matt green foliage and small white flower spikes — looks just like a juniper. *H. salicornoides,* 18 in. by 3 ft., yellow-green conifer-like foliage. These two are hardier than the types grown for flowers.

**Ground cover** There is one really outstanding plant here, *H. pinguifolia* 'Pagei', 1 ft. by 3 ft., small rounded leaves of a good blue-grey all the year; flowers white, not good. Excellent ground cover and a good background for other plants. Plant in groups. Layers; half-ripe cuttings.

# *Helianthemum* / Sun rose

Mat-forming shrubs with small, oval glossy leaves and richly colored florin-size flowers. Hot, dry positions. Single-flowered types are most charming, but the flowers are very short-lived. Double-flowered types hold their flowers for three or four days, instead of one day only, and have a much longer flowering season. June till autumn. Trim over with shears after flowering to keep neat. Dozens of named varieties in every shade of red, yellow, pink, orange and white, some have variegated foliage. Select as available. Single varieties increase by seed or layers; double varieties by layers or half-ripe cuttings.

Heathers are most effective in flower when massed. Several types will grow on alkaline or limestone soils.

## *Helichrysum*

*H. petiolatum* is grown for its gay grey lavender-like foliage topped with sprays of bright yellow flowers in July. Plant in spring. Full sun, best on sandy soils. Cut back to old wood after four or five years. Half-ripe cuttings. Tender.

## *Hypericum*/St. John's wort

(See also Deciduous Shrubs.) The most useful member of this genus is *H. calycinum,* growing to 18 in., bright brown stems and 2½-in. bright yellow flowers; it makes excellent ground cover in full sun, flowers all summer and autumn. Suckers; division.

## *Ilex*/Holly

Most of the hollies ultimately form very tall shrubs indeed, but are slow growing. All the following are forms of the English holly, *I. aquifolium.* Females carry the berries, and need a male to pollinate them, unless otherwise stated. 'Argentea Marginata', broad, silver-margined leaves, bushy habit, free-fruiting; 'Golden King', leaves green with a bright gold margin and few spines, male; 'Pyramidalis', dense growth, very free fruiting, self-fertile; 'Argenteomarginata Pendula' (Perry's weeping silver holly), a gracefully weeping holly with silver-margined leaves: very free fruiting. Cut out any branches that produce entirely green leaves — otherwise no pruning. Half-ripe cuttings, July/August, very slow to root; layers when convenient. Japanese and Chinese hollies are also useful.

## *Kalmia*/Mountain Laurel

Closely related to rhododendrons, and like them needing acid soil and plenty of peat or leaf-mold in the soil: will withstand more sun than rhododendrons. Best known is *K. latifolia,* 6 ft. by 5 ft., flat heads of neat pentagonal pink flowers with deeper pink spots. Seedlings are variable in depth of color. *K. angustifolia,* 2 ft., forms a dense, slowly suckering shrub with deep pink flowers and bronze winter foliage, useful at the front of a border. Seed; suckers.

## *Lavendula*/Lavender

Always popular, this does best on light, sandy soil in full sun. Grey leaves, spikes of strongly scented lavender flowers. All parts of the shrub are aromatic. Old English lavender is *L. officinalis,* 3 ft. by 3 ft., flowering July-September, most widely grown; 'Nana Compacta' is the French lavender, with darker flowers and a dwarfer habit. Trim over with shears to keep neat. Old, leggy plants should be thrown out and new ones planted. Cuttings root easily at any season. Seed is easy, but seedlings vary in color and vigor.


## *Lupinus*/Tree lupin

*L. arboreus* is a short-lived shrub to about 8 ft. by 4 ft., fresh green trifoliate leaves and pale yellow or whitish lupin flowers May/June, scented. Dead-head but do not prune. Good temporary gap-fillers, but little permanent use. Seed. For mild climates.


## *Mahonia*

Attractive and useful evergreens with spine-edged pinnate leaves and clusters of yellow lily-of-the-valley like flowers in winter or early spring. The commonest is *M. aquifolium,* 4 ft. by 4 ft., yellow flowers followed by black berries with a blue bloom; some of the leaves turn claret in winter. Forms a dense, slowly suckering shrub excellent in sun or shade, will grow in dense shade; 'Atropurpurea' has purple foliage. *M. bealei* is similar but more handsome. *M.* × 'Charity' is finest of all, with a stately, upright habit, bold, architectural foliage and very large clusters of very deep yellow flowers from February or March, 6 ft. by 4 ft. Half-ripe cuttings; suckers where applicable.


## *Osmanthus*

*O. fortunei* and *O. heterophyllus,* 7 ft. by 6 ft., are outstanding: deep green leaves and masses of ½-in. tubular white sweetly scented flowers in April. Highly effective. Any soil, full sun; hardy to Washington, D.C. Layers; half-ripe cuttings — but very slow to root.

The mountain laurel or calico bush *Kalmia latifolia* is closely related to rhododendrons. It needs the same sort of soil but will stand more sun.

Hollies may be grown not only for their Christmas-time berries but also for the glossy leaves of many types. Only female plants produce berries. A Chinese holly is shown.

## Pernettya

Superb evergreen carpeting ground-cover shrubs strictly for acid soil, producing masses of brightly colored berries which last all through winter. Useful where temperature not lower than 10°F. *P. mucronata,* 3 ft. spreading, needed for pollinating female forms. The best forms are 'Bell's Seedling', large dark red berries; 'Davies Hybrids', berries in various shades of pink, all good; 'White', large white berries. No pruning. Suckers.

## *Phormium*/New Zealand flax

Grown for their erect, sword-like leaves rather than their flowers which are curious but not lovely. Grown in warm areas, they seem to suffer more from damp, mild winters than hard ones. *P. tenax,* clump forming to 8 ft. tall, leaves green; 'Purpureum', smaller growing, leaves deepest bronze-purple; 'Varietgatum', leaves with a creamy white margin; 'Veitchii', leaves striped yellow. The two variegated forms are more tender than the green-leaved or purple forms. *P. colensoi* is smaller growing and hardier, to about 3 ft.; 'Bronze Boy' is a useful dwarf with deep coppery-purple leaves to 18 in. Any soil; best in sun. Division; seed in heat.

## *Phlomis*/Jerusalem Sage

*P. fruiticosa,* 2 ft. by 4 ft., grey sage-like leaves and whorls of hooded yellow flowers June/July. Does best in hot, dry positions. Half-ripe cuttings.

## *Pieris*/Andromeda

Strictly for acid soils and shade: very spectacular. Flowers white, bell-shaped, produced in clusters like lily-of-the-valley. The finest of all is *P. forrestii,* 8 ft. by 6 ft., grown not so much for its flowers as for its young leaves which come through brilliant scarlet in the manner of a poinsettia, and gradually fade through pinks to yellows before turning green in late summer; leaves pointed, oval, matt. Flowers appear with the scarlet new leaves. Needs overhead tree protection from late frosts. *P. japonica* is the best for flower, being smothered in blossom in March/April. *P. taiwanensis* is similar but has the additional merit of good bright copper young foliage; seeds itself freely in conditions that suit it. All need plenty of peat or leaf-mold in the soil, and shade. Layers; half-ripe cuttings, August. Seed is easy but the plants hybridize readily; hybrids can be very good. *P. japonica* 'Variegata' is a very small, slow-growing form with a white variegation: good, but the flowers are lost against the variegated foliage. Various supposedly 'pink' forms are, so far, hardly worth bothering with.

## *Piptanthus*/Evergreen laburnum

*P. laburnifolius,* once grown only as a wall-shrub, is well adapted to the South, 8 ft. by 4 ft. Greyish trifoliate leaves and upright spikes of pineapple-scented laburnum-like flowers, deep yellow, April-June. Usually short-lived. Any soil; sun. Seed.

## *Pyracantha*/Firethorn

An excellent hedge plant, and ideal for covering a north or east wall, these will grow well in the open garden, perfectly hardy. Grown for its enormous crops of orange, yellow or red berries in the fall. *P. coccinea* 'Lalandii' is the commonest species. *P. rogersiana* has whiter flowers and can be bought in forms with red, orange or yellow berries. Half-ripe cuttings, August.

## *Rhododendron*

A huge genus of shrubs needing acid soil and mostly some shade. There are over 500 hardy species and several thousand hybrids. Enthusiasts should consult specialized books. Only the briefest selection can be given here. All need a soil enriched with peat or leaf-mold. The majority of plants offered, especially by garden centers, are known as 'hardy hybrids'. Two excellent ones are 'Pink Pearl', a large growing typically rhododendron-like rhododendron with huge candy-floss pink flowers and 'Brittania', with a rather spreading habit, rather yellowish, matt leaves, and flowers of a red, somewhat compounded with blue — a very impure color. Much better is 'May Day', with smaller leaves, matt green above, orange felted beneath and pure scarlet flowers very freely produced. Other good reds are 'Cynthia', 'Doncaster', 'John Waterer' and 'Lord Roberts'. The best of the pinks include 'Betty Wormald', coral pink with a striking deep chocolate blotch; 'Gomer Waterer', blush pink with a yellow eye; and 'Souvenir of Dr. Endtz', a deeper, richer color than 'Pink Pearl'. The best purples include 'Blue Peter', pale lavander-blue; 'fatsuosum flore pleno', a double purple; and 'Purple Splendour', rich purple with black markings. Good whites include 'Sappho', pure white with a

The mahonias are attractive both in leaf and flower. Most produce their flowers in winter or early spring when there is little else in flower in the garden.

striking dark eye; 'Cunningham's White', earlier than most, pure white, spotted; and 'Diane', creamy white shaded primrose. Apart from the 'hardy hybrids' there are a number of very exciting new hybrids, many of them not looking at all like the traditional old hardy hybrids. Some of the best of these are 'St. Tudy', with willowy leaves and pure blue flowers in enormous profusion; 'Lady Chamberlain', with dangling orange bells and bluish spring foliage and 'Temple Belle' with round leaves and tubby little pink flowers. These need more shade than the hardy hybrids. All the above grow to about 8 ft. by 8 ft. There are a number of very useful dwarf rhododendrons, some of the most easily obtainable of which are 'Blue Diamond', the brightest and purest blue of the small-leaved blue hybrids, ultimately forming a narrow column about 8 ft. by 3 ft., will grow in full sun; 'Elizabeth', a small, beehive-shaped shrub with medium-sized leaves and huge bright red flowers, about 3 ft. by 4 ft., needs shelter from early morning sunlight; 'Creeping Jenny' is similar but sprawls about on the ground and has more orange in the flower, 2 ft. spreading indefinitely but slowly. *R. praecox,* the earliest flowering of the small species, delicate mauve flowers in March, very striking, 5 ft. by 4 ft. *R. williamsianum,* 4 ft. by 3 ft., round leaves, copper new leaves and tubby pink bells. There are other really worthwhile rhododendrons that may not be quite so easy to obtain: 'Fabia' is one of the best of these, a hybrid with brilliant orange flowers; 'Hawk var. Crest' is the finest of all the large-growing yellows; while 'Remo' is the finest of the small-leaved yellows. *R. augustinii* is, in its finest forms, the bluest of all rhododendrons, though it may not look like a rhododendron to the uninitiated. Very variable from seed. Rhododendrons need no routine pruning but should be dead-headed after flowering. An annual mulch with peat or leaf-mold helps to keep them growing well. Layering.

## *Rosmarinus*/Rosemary

Aromatic shrub whose leaves have culinary uses, it is grown mainly for its grey foliage, the aroma it gives off in hot weather and hardly at all for its insignificant bluish flowers. Rather an ugly, straggly plant, 4 ft. by 4 ft. Sun; any soil. Half-ripe cuttings, July/August. Hardy in mild, frost-free areas.

# *Ruta*/Rue

*R. graveolens* is grown for its charmingly divided blue foliage. 3 ft., spreading slowly. Cut back hard in spring to keep tidy. Sun; any soil. Soft cuttings with a heel in May.

# *Santolina*/Cotton lavender

Low-growing shrubs with good grey foliage. *S. chamaecyparissus,* 2 ft. by 4 ft., dense, neat habit, saw-edged leaves, yellow daisy-type flowers June-August. Best in a light, sandy soil. Cut back hard each spring to keep neat, otherwise becomes straggly. Cuttings at any season.

# *Sarcococca*

Useful ground-cover plants for grouping in the shade. The best is *S. hookeriana humilis* a little plant to 2 ft. by 3 ft., with narrow dark green leaves and small white strongly scented flowers in February. Any soil; sun or shade. Suckers; division.

# *Senecio*

A huge genus embracing over 1,300 plants, some woody, some herbaceous, including the common weed groundsel. The shrubby members are mainly good evergreys, particularly useful by the seaside. All do best in a sandy soil in full sun. Two are outstanding: *S. cineraria* 'White Diamond', 2 ft. by 3 ft., beautifully lobed leaves covered in bright white wool. Often planted as annual plants for foliage effect. *S. laxifolius* has white felted oval leaves, 3 ft. by 5 ft. Prune hard each spring. Soft cuttings of the latter, cuttings at any season of the first. Not common in the U.S.

# *Skimmia*

Neat berry-bearing evergreens with oval, glossy leaves, rather slow growing. Both males and females need to be planted to obtain berries. The best is *S. japonica,* the female bearing glowing red berries that do not seem to be much liked by birds and last all winter. The male bears deep pink buds opening to pale pink clusters of sweetly scented flowers in spring. Do not do well on limestone soils; no pruning. Half-ripe cuttings, July/August.

# Viburnum

(See also Deciduous Shrubs.) Several evergreen viburnums are well worth growing. One is a large plant, to 10 ft. by 7 ft., with 9-in. felted leaves, large flat clusters of whitish flowers in May/June and large clusters of red berries in winter known as *V. rhytidophyllum.* Another, *V. davidii,* is a dense, spreading shrub, 3 ft. by 5 ft. at the most, with polished oval leaves with deep linear veins; flowers insignificant, but the female bears brilliant turquoise berries all through winter; plant one male to every three females. Best when grouped closely. Layers or half-ripe cuttings.

# Vinca/Periwinkle

All make dense ground cover, even in shade, though they flower best in full sun. The lesser periwinkle. *V. minor,* has small blue starry flowers from mid-summer till frosts. This is the hardiest of the 2 species. There are many forms: 'Aureo-variegata' has bright golden variegation; 'Variegata' has a silver variegation; 'Bowles' Variety' is the deepest blue; 'Alba' has white flowers and is good in shade; there is also a double form. *V. major* is altogether a larger plant, both in leaf and flower, it flowers mainly in May, producing a few flowers sporadically through the rest of the year. Flowers bright blue, 1 in. across; 'Maculata' has light red stems and leaves whose centers are splashed with gold. Trim over with shears to keep neat. Increase by division.

# Yucca

Striking plants with usually rigid sword-shaped leaves of bold, architectural appearance, rather tropical-looking and huge spikes of creamy white bells. The finest of all is *Y. gloriosa,* sometimes known as Spanish dagger, it forms a rather meandering trunk up to 6 ft. on top of which sits a rosette of sharply pointed leaves. *Y. recurvifolia* is similar, but the older leaves bend downwards. Both have viciously rigid, pointed tips to their leaves, best avoided, particularly if there are children about. The freest-flowering species is *Y. filamentosa,* Adams needle, a stemless, clump-forming shrub with soft recurving leaves and softer tips to the leaves; these are edged with white, hanging threads, 2 ft. Flowers to 4 ft., white, flowers in July. The hardiest of the species. There is a striking variegated form. *Y. flaccida* is similar, with the leaves appearing to have been broken half-way along their length. Not quite so free in flower. Pull off dead leaves. Increase by offsets; seed. Generally hardy south of Washington, D.C.

# 9 Conifers

Conifers, especially the smaller growing species and many of the dwarf forms, have an important part to play in the shrub garden, though this does not seem to have been widely appreciated. They are particularly valuable for the contrast they afford with broad-leaved shrubs, both deciduous and evergreen, and many are treasured because of their colored growths.

Conifers are woody perennials that bear cones — a very misleading definition — since a great many, like the yew *Taxus baccata* bear brightly colored fruits. The important thing about them botanically is that they evolved long before flowering plants.

All those described here are evergreen, though not all conifers are evergreen. Evergreen is perhaps a misnomer, since colors vary from light green to black-green, while others are blue, gold, silver, bronze and even rosy-red. In addition to the colorfulness of their foliage they are useful too, for their variety of shapes, ranging from the narrowly columnar Irish juniper *Juniperus communis hibernica* to the completely prostrate ground-covering *Juniperus sabina tamariscifolia*.

Most can be raised from cuttings placed in a cold frame; they are, however, slow to root and in general it is better to buy healthy plants from nurseries. Plant in spring and protect from cold winds. Water freely their first year, and keep a good mulch over the roots. Relatively free from pests and diseases, their greatest enemy is dogs!

All the conifers described here are suitable for smaller gardens.

## *Abies*/Fir

*A. koreana* is suitable for smaller gardens, very slowly growing to about 15 ft. by 8 ft. Compact, stiffly branches, with relatively broad needles densely arranged all around the twigs, green on top, white beneath; cones erect, candle-like.

# *Chamaecyparis*/False cypress

Differ from *Cupressus* in their mainly tiny cones, otherwise similar. *C. obtusa gracilis nana*, foliage bright green arranged in curious whorls, dense growth, 3 ft. by 2 ft. *C. lawsoniana* 'Ellwoodii', very popular, narrowly columnar with feathery glaucous foliage; grows quickly to about 6 ft. by 2 ft., but much more slowly once it has reached that height. *C.l.* 'Minima Aurea', has ascending branches and branchlets which twist sideways to reveal the soft, golden foliage edge-ways on; dense growth 3 ft. by 2 ft. *C.l.* 'Glauca' striking bluish foliage, broadly conical habit, 3 ft. by 3 ft. *C.l.* 'Tharandtensis Caesia', 5 ft. by 4 ft., blue-green leaves turn bronze with age; prune back long shoots; not good on limestone soils. *C.l. obtusa* 'Pygmea', a low, spreading bush, wider than high, reaching about 2 ft., with flat, fan-shaped branches and foliage in tiers one on top of the other; foliage bronzy colored when mature. *C. pisifera* 'Boulevard', 4 ft. by 4 ft., striking silvery-blue foliage, bushy, rounded habit; withstands pruning well if need arises to keep it to size; best in light shade; not good on limestone soils. *C.p.* 'Filifera Aurea', 3 ft. by 3 ft., slowly forms a broadly cone-shaped shrub with drooping, thread-like branchlets with golden foliage; unusual and striking. *C.p.* 'Plumosa Aurea Nana', 18 in. by 18 in., a dense, conical shrub with soft yellow foliage, particularly good in spring. *C. thyoides* 'Ericoides', 4 ft. by 3 ft., forms a very close-growing, compact pyramidal shrub with permanently juvenile feathery foliage of dark grey-green in summer, turning plum-purple or violet in winter. Needs protection from cold winter winds.

# *Juniperus*/Juniper

A large genus of tough, hardy plants, very variable in habit and general appearance.

**Prostrate varieties** *J. communis* 'Depressa Aurea', a wide-spreading shrub up to 2 ft. tall but much wider, leaves golden yellow in early summer, later turning bronze. *J.c.* 'Hornbrookii', 6 to 9 in tall, 3 to 4 ft. across, completely prostrate but gradually forming a mound in the center; tiny leaves and very neat habit; young growth green, later turning copper. *J.c.* 'Repanda', 1 ft. by 4 ft., completely prostrate and good ground cover, mounding slightly in the center with age; foliage sprays are sometimes flat, sometimes turned on edge, making a curious effect. *F. horizantalis* 'Glauca', 9 in., spreading indefinitely but slowly, permanently prostrate, mat-forming, with long straight branches densely covered in blue-green leaves. *J. sabina tamariscifolia*, the Spanish juniper, 1 ft. by 4 ft., dense, prostrate habit and good ground cover, the branches building up in layers, feathery bright green foliage.

**Spreading varieties** *J. chinensis* 'Plumosa Aurea', 4 ft. by 3 ft., branches held upwards and outwards, drooping at the tips, thickly covered in green and yellow foliage. *J. chinensis* 'Pfitzeriana', 6 ft. by 6 ft., branches are produced at 45°, foliage greyish green, always popular. *J.c.* 'Aurea', similar to the above but with golden foliage which turns a rich bronzy color in winter.

**Erect varieties** *J. chinensis* 'Albovariegata', 8 ft. by 3 ft., dense conical habit, glaucous foliage splashed with white. *J.c.* 'Pyramidalis' ('Stricta'), 8 ft. by 4 ft., vividly glaucous rigid juvenile foliage, very striking. *J. communis* 'Compressa', 15 in. by 6 in., one of the best of the real dwarfs, cone-shaped with very dense blue-grey foliage.

# *Picea*/Spruce

*P. glauca albertiana,* 4 ft. by 3 ft., slow growing, a perfectly symmetrical true cone; foliage very dense; particularly lovely in spring with its fresh green needles. *P. abris,* Norway Spruce, is available in many forms. Generally a tall growing species. *P. a. nidiformis,* 2 ft. by 2 ft., is a rather shapeless bush, often offered; it tends to die off in the center.

# *Pinus*/Pine trees

*P. mugo* is a charming dwarf decidely shrubby species, 3 ft. by 3 ft. *P.m.* 'Pumilo', 2 ft. by 2 ft., is similar but smaller still. Both bear miniature cones, both are very hardy, and both are excellent on dry or sandy banks.

# *Taxus*/Yew

*T. baccata* 'Standishii' is the finest for small gardens, forming a very narrow upright little tree with gay golden-yellow leaves; slow growing to about 10 ft. by 1 ft. *T.b.* 'Nana' is one of the real miniatures, forming a typical yew-shaped tree but in miniature, reaching about 1 ft. by 9 in. in 25 years. *T. canadensis,* Canada yew is one of the hardiest, useful as a ground cover plant.

# *Thuya*

*T. occidentalis* 'Holmstrup', 8 ft. by 4 ft., slowly forms a narrowly conical bush with vertical sprays of rich green foliage. *T.o.* 'Rheingold', 4 ft. by 3 ft., forms an almost round bush with bright russet foliage deepening to bronze in autumn and gold in winter.

# 10 Shrubs & Decorative Evergreens

Anyone who has read the foregoing descriptive lists will have noticed that certain shrubs do better in some soils and situations than in others. This can be frustrating if you do not happen to have the conditions that the one shrub you most want to grow happens to need — i.e. acid soil and shade. On the other hand, there is another way of looking at this: see what soil and conditions you have, see what will grow in those conditions, and then set out to make the best combination you can.

The lists given here are not exhaustive, but should be helpful.

*Symbols:* **BLE,** *Broadleaf evergreen;* **D,** *deciduous;* **C,** *Conifer;* **Height,** *Average maximum height.*

*Abelia grandiflora*     Glossy Abelia     **BLE** 5'
Flowers white to light pink, July to frost, foliage bronze in the fall.
*Abies koreana*     Korean Fir     **C.** 50'
Slow growing, compact, needles white beneath
*Acer japonica*     Fullmoon Maple     **D** 25'
Trees with 7 to 11 lobes per leaf, green turning red in the fall, several forms; cv. 'Aureum' - leaves yellow green; cv. 'Laciniatum' - leaves deeply lobed and toothed.
*Acer palmatum*     Japanese Maple     **D** 15'
About 80 cultivars of this species, leaves varying from 5 to 11 lobes, colored forms best in light shade; cv. 'Atropurpureum' reddish foliage throughout the year; cv. 'Dissectum' (Threadleaf) green foliage, red in fall; cv. 'Dissectum atropurpureum' red foliage throughout the year; cv. 'Osakazuki,' large leaves yellowish green, brilliant red in fall.
*Aralia chinensis*     Chinese Angelica Tree     **D** 20'
Large leaves to 3 ft., white flowers in August, cv. 'Aurea Marginata' with gold variegation in leaves; cv. 'Argentea Marginata' with silver variegation.
*Arbutus unedo*     Strawberry Tree     **BLE** 20'
Slow growing, for mild climates, white flowers in Nov.-Dec. followed by orange fruit, edible but tasteless.

*Artemesia arbotanum*    Southern Wormwood    **D** 4'
  Grown for silvery grey foliage, cut to ground each spring for fresh stems and foliage, for mild climates.

*Aucuba japonica*    Japanese Aucuba    **BLE** 15'
  Glossy thick leaves, grow in partial shade, several variegated forms, red fruits on female plants in late winter-early spring.

*Berberis*    Barberry
  Many species and cultivars, thorny shrubs with generally red, bluish or black fruits, deciduous and evergreen kinds.

*B. buxifolia nana*    Dwarf Magellan Barberry    **BLE** 1½-2'
  Excellent for dwarf hedges, leaves to 1 inch long, very hardy.

*B. darwin*    Darwin Barberry    **BLE** 8 to 10'
  Autumn foliage purplish, holly-like leaves, orange-red flowers, purplish fruit in fall.

*B. julianae*    Wintergreen Barberry    **BLE** 6'
  Spiny leaves, bluish-black berries, vigorous grower.

*B. korean*    Korean Barberry    **D** 6'
  Somewhat similar to Japanese Barberry, red fruits, foliage red in fall, growth dense.

*B. mentorensis*    Mentor Barberry    **BLE** 7'
  A hybrid of the Wintergreen barberry and Japanese Barberry, tolerates drought situations, spiny leaves, may be semi-evergreen under adverse winter conditions.

*B. stenophylla*    Rosemary Barberry    **BLE** 8'
  A hybrid of Darwin Barberry and *B. empetrifolia,* graceful arching branches with dense habit of growth.

*B. thunbergii*    Japanese Barberry    **D** 6'
  Excellent dense-growth shrub, tolerates poor soil and dry conditions, use in sun or light shade, several cultivars: 'Atropurpurea' with bronze red foliage; cv. 'Crimson Pygmy' a dwarf red leaf form; cv. 'Minor' dwarf' with very small leaves.

*B. verruculosa*    Warty Barberry    **BLE** 4'
  Leaves leathery, dark green, white below, arching branches, dark blue to black berries in fall, autumn foliage bronze.

*Buddleia alternifolia*    Fountain Buddleia    **D** 15'
  Arching branches, flowers small lilac purple in May - June, flowers produced on previous years growth, prune out oldest stems after flowering.

*B. davidii*    Butterfly Bush    **D** 15'
  Long upright branches, killed to the ground in cold climates or prune each spring to induce new growth, flowers in July-Aug. on current seasons growth, flowers white, pink, red or purple in terminal panicles, popular cultivars include 'Peace' - white  'Ile de France' - purple and 'Royal Red'.

*Callicarpa americana*    American Beauty-berry    **D** 6'
For mild climates, native in S. E. U. S., open habit of growth, garden value mainly for purple berries in fall after leaf drop.

*C. japonica*    Japanese Beauty-berry    **D** 4'
Upright growth, foliage yellow in fall, drops early, berries violet to purple, may be pruned severely each year as flowers are borne on current seasons growth.

*Calluna vulgaris*    Heather    **BLE** 1½'
Grow in moist acid soil, low fertility, plant in full sun, in cold climate mulch with coarse material, prune in early spring, flowers white, pink or reddish in late summer.

*Camellia japonica*    Camellia    **BLE** to 20'
Shrubs to small trees for sun or partial shade, tolerates winter temperatures to about 10°F, acid soil with organic matter, prune in early spring only to keep plant in form, flowers single to several forms of doubles, white, pink, red or bicolored, Nov. to March, several hundred cultivars.

*C. sasanqua*    Sasanqua or Fall Camellia    **BLE** 20'
Plant open in habit, foliage smaller than common camellia, flowers single to semi-double, white or pink, culture and hardiness same as for common camellia.

*Caryopteris clandonensis*    Bluebeard    **D** 4'
A hybrid of *C. incana* and *C. mongholica* with gray green foliage, spikes of blue flowers in late summer, plant in full sun, prune severely each spring to produce stronger shoots and larger flowers. Cv. 'Blue Mist'.

*Ceanothus delilianus*    Delisle Ceanothus    **D** 6'
A hybrid of *C. americana* and *C. coeruleus,* deciduous to semi-evergreen, blue flowers, several cultivars, especially adaptable on west coast, tolerates mild winters.

*C. thyrsiflorous*    Blue Blossom or California Lilac    **BLE** 25'
Native to Pacific coast, tolerates temperatures to 10°F, blue flowers in spring.

*Ceratostigma plumbaginoides*    Leadwort    **D** 1'
A ground cover plant, killed to ground by frost, useful in sun or partial shade, flowers in July to frost, foliage reddish bronze in fall.

*C. willmottianum*    Blue Leadwort    **D.** 4'
A small shrub suitable for California and Gulf states, tolerates poor soil, blue phlox-like flowers in summer to frost.

*Chaenomeles speciosa*    Flowering Quince    **D** 6'
Excellent spring flowering shrub, flowers white, pink, orange or red, dense habit of growth, glossy foliage, somewhat thorny, fruits yellow green to green.

*Chamaecyparis lawsoniana*    Lawson False Cypress.    **C**
Many forms of this large tree native to California and Oregon,
Cv. 'Ellwoodii', dense bluish color; cv. 'Lutea', yellow foliage turning
golden yellow; cv. 'Minima', dwarf and compact.
*C. obtusa*    Hinoki False Cypress    **C**
Dwarf forms of this slow growing Japanese species, very hardy; cv.
'Nana' one of the dwarfest of evergreens,; cv. 'Nana Gracilis', dark
green foliage to 4'; cv. 'Pygmaea', fan shaped branchlets, bronzy-green.
*C. pisifera*    Sawara False Cypress    **C**
Small growing forms of this large tree native to Japan are used. cv.
'Boulevard' (Cyanoviridis) light blue foliage, one of the best of the
"blue" evergreens; cv. 'Filifera' with long thread like branches; cv.
'Filifera Aurea' similar except with yellow green foliage; cv. 'Squarrosa'
bluish green foliage soft, moss like to touch.
*Chiamonathus praecox*    Wintersweet    **D** 8 to 10'
Late winter flowering shrub with fragrant yellow flowers, leaves
yellow in fall, an open habit of growth.
*Chionanthus virginicus*    Fringe Tree    **D** 30'
A small tree with white flowers in loose panicles in May blue fruit in
clusters, foliage yellow in fall.
*Cistus*    Rockrose    **BLE** 2' to 4'
Several species and hybrids, suitable for mild climates, plant in
sunny locations, transplant as small pot-grown plants.
*Cornus*    Dogwood    **D**
An important genus of shrubs and small trees adaptable to all parts of
the country.
*C. alba*    Siberian Dogwood    **D** 8'
Vigorous growing, clusters of yellowish white flowers in spring,
foliage red in fall, stems bright red the first year of growth, prune out
oldest stems each spring to have new growth.
*C. alternifolia*    Alternate Leaf Dogwood    **D.** 20'
A small tree, flowers in clusters like Viburnum, in May, bluish-
black berries in fall, cv. 'Argentea' has variegated leaves.
*C. florida*    Flowering Dogwood    **D** 30'
Best native small flowering tree, plant in full sun or partial shade,
showy part of flower is a bract, white, pink or red, also double flowered
types, cv. 'Pluribracteata' - double; cv. 'Fastigata' - upright form; cv.
'Pendula' - weeping form; new cultivars include 'Cherokee Chief' - ruby
red; 'Appleblossom' - light pink and 'White Cloud.'
*C. kousa*    Japanese Dogwood    **D** 20'
Flowers 3 to 4 weeks after Flowering Dogwood, bracts pointed and
fruit is in raspberry-like clusters, fall foliage red.

*C. mas*    Cornelian Cherry    **D** 15'
Yellow flowers in Feb. - March, very hardy, grows as a shrub or small tree, fruit red, cherry like, edible.

*C. nuttallii*    Pacific Dogwood    **D** 50'
Bracts 4 to 6 per flower, white to light pink in April, native in Pacific Northwest, grows poorly outside of the mild moist climate of that area.

*C. stolenifera (C. serices)*    Red Osier Dogwood    **D** 6'
A multistemmed shrub with red stems in winter, useful in wet locations, creeping stems, also a yellow stemmed form, 'Flaviramea' and green stem form 'Nitida'.

*Corylopsis spicata*    Winterhazel    **D** 6'
Early spring flowering, yellow flowers in drooping spikes, bud or flowers may be killed by late frost.

*Corylus avellana*    European Hazel    **D** 15'
Cultivars of the hazelnut have garden plant value, cv. 'Contorta', twigs curled and twisted to 10' tall, cv. 'Aurea' with yellow green leaves, cv. 'Pendula' pendulous branches and a weeping form if grafted high on understock.

*C. maxima purpurea*    Purple Filbert    **D** 15' to 20'
Grown in full sun for the dark purple foliage.

*Cotinus coggygria*    Smokebush    **D** 15'
Planted for its pinkish fruiting panicles in late summer, grow in full sun, foliage bronze red in fall, slow to become established.

*Cotoneaster adpressa*    Creeping Cotoneaster    **D** 8'
Slow growing, pink flowers in June, red fruit, excellent for rock gardens.

*C. dammeri*    Bearberry Cotoneaster    **BLE** 1'
Ground cover for moist soil areas, roots along the stem, may lose leaves in very cold weather, bright green foliage.

*C. franchetii*    Franchet Cotoneaster    **D to Semi-Ev.** 10'
Upright shrub, fruit orange red, reddish foliage in fall.

*C. horizontalis*    Rock Spray    **D. to Semi-Ev.** 2'
Flat horizontal habit of growth, bright red berries in fall, effectively espaliered on a wall.

*C. microphylla*    Small leaved Cotoneaster    **BLE** 3'
Small leaves, compact growth habit, excellent as a specimen or in a rock garden.

*C. salicifolia floccosa*    Willowleaf Cotoneaster    **Semi-Ev.** 10'
Best in mild climates, graceful arching habit of growth, underside of leaves densely hairy.

*C. zabelei*    Cherryberry Cotoneaster    **D** 6'
Spreading branches, dense habit of growth, foliage yellow in fall.

*Cytisus scoparius*    Scotch Broom    **D** 6'
The most widely planted species of this plant in the United States. Flowers yellow, pea-like in May-June, stems green throughout the year, prefers acid soil, little pruning required.

*Daphne burkwoodii*    Burkwood Daphne    **BLE** 6'
Fragrant white to pink flowers in early spring, vigorous growing.

*D. mezereum*    February Daphne    **D** 3'
Rosy purple flowers in spring before foliage, red berries in June.

*D. odoro*    Winter Daphne    **BLE** 4'
Very fragrant white flowers in March, tolerates temperatures to about 10°F, plant in partial shade, also a variegated yellow and green form.

*Deutzia gracilis*    Slender Deutzia    **D** 6'
White single flowers in May - June, graceful small shrub.

*D. scabra*    Pride of Rochester    **D** 8'
An excellent double-flowered form of this species, flowers rosy pink to white, last of the deutzias to flower, June-July, tolerates city conditions.

*Elaeagnus pungens*    Thorny Elaeagnus    **BLE** 10'
Variegated forms as 'Aureus', 'Tricolor' and 'Variegatus' add color in the garden, tolerates mild winters, flowers in Oct.-Nov., fragrant.

*Erica carnea*    Spring Heath    **BLE** 1'
Related to *Calluna* (Heather), requiring an acid soil and full sun, flowers in later winter, early spring, white, pink and red, use in mass planting for effectiveness.

*Euonymus alatus*    Winged Euonymus    **D** 8'
Valued for its interesting winged bark on branches, brilliant red fall color.

*E. fortunei*    Wintercreeper    **BLE** 1'
Also known as *E. radicans,* use as a vine or ground cover, many forms varying in leaf size, variegated white or yellow green foliage, upright habit of growth or forms with purplish bronze foliage in the fall.

*Exochordia racemosa*    Pearlbush    **D** 8'
Spring flowering, white blooms, borne on previous years growth.

*Fatshedera lizei*    Fatshedera    **BLE** 6'
Glossy green leaves, texture similar to English Ivy, satisfactory only in mild climates, or as a house plant.

*Forsythia*    Forsythia or Golden Bells    **D**
Easily grown and generally pest free plants, all early spring flowering, prune old wood after flowering, several species and hybrids, recommended cultivars include 'Beatrix Farrand', large vivid yellow flowers; cv. 'Lynwood', brilliant yellow flowers, upright habit of growth; cv. 'Spectabilis', vivid yellow flowers in abundance, upright; cv. 'Bronxen-

sis', developed from *F. viridissima,* dwarf, 2 ft., spreading, yellow flowers small.

*Fuchsia hybrida*    Common Fuchsia    **BLE** 3 - 4'

Suitable in frost free areas, used in the north as summer garden or pot plants, many cultivars and species.

*F. megellanica*    Magellan Fuchsia    **Semi-Ev.** 3'

Flowers red and violet, in mid to late summer, plant in a protected area, cv. 'Riccartonii' is the hardiest form for the garden.

*Hamamelis mollis*    Chinese Witch-hazel    **D** 5'

Late winter flowering shrubs, golden, yellowish to reddish fragrant flowers, hybrids of this species and *H. japonica* have larger flowers often copper or reddish colors and are called *H. intermedia.*

*Helianthemum nummularium*    Sun Rose    **BLE** 1'

Low-growing plants for full sun and in mild climates, require winter production where temperatures to 20°F or lower, flowers white, pink, yellow in June and during the summer.

*Hibiscus syriacus*    Shrub Althea    **D.** 15'

Late summer flowering shrubs, upright habit of growth, tolerates seaside conditions, late to produce leaves in the spring, flowers single, semi-double and double, 2½ to 4'' diameter, colors white, pink, red to purple blue.

*Hydrangea arborescens*    Smooth Hydrangea    **D** 3'

The form grandiflora called Hills of Snow is most commonly grown with large white flower clusters in June-July, prune in early spring.

*H. macrophylla*    Bigleaf or Florists Hydrangea    **D** 3'

This is most frequently grown as a spring flowering greenhouse plant, many cultivars of these greenhouse types are not winter hardy in temperatures below 20°F in winter, when flower buds are filled cv. 'Otaksa' is widely grown and more hardy than greenhouse types.

*H. paniculata grandiflora*    Peegee Hydrangea    **D** 20'

Late with large pinkish flower panicles 10 to 15'' long turning brown and remaining on the plant into winter, plants may become small trees.

*Hypericum patulum*    St. Johns Wort    **D** 3'

Yellow flowers to 2½'' diameter in mid summer to frost, plant in full sun, well drained soil, leaves red in fall, cv. 'Hidcote' flowers golden yellow, fragrant, in cold winters may kill to ground while in the southern states it may be evergreen.

*Ilex*    Holly

Many species and cultivars, one of the most valuable of woody plants, grow in acid soil, plants dioecious, red berried kinds most showy, several interspecific hybrids.

*I. aquifolium*    English Holly    **BLE** 50'

Suitable to areas where winter temperatures do not go below 5°F, glossy green foliage, shapes varying with cultivar, red berries, many cultivars, variegated forms with either white or yellow markings.

*I. cornuta*    Chinese Holly    **BLE** 6 - 8'

Glossy green leaves, squarish at ends, cv. 'Burfordii', leaves generally without spines, fruits heavily, compact forms, rounded growth, without fruit.

*I. crenata*    Japanese Holly    **BLE** variable

Many selections and cultivars, fruit black, not showy, cv. 'Microphylla' with small leaves; cv. 'convexa' generally rounded, compact, a substitute for Boxwood in cold climates; cv. 'Helleri', dwarf compact to 3 to 4'; cv. 'Kingsville Green Cushion', very dwarf to 1' and broad spreading.

*I. opaca*    American Holly    **BLE** 50'

American species hardy to 5°F, many cultivars, use as a specimen tree or hedge, fruit red although there are white forms as well as yellow and ivory.

*I. verticillata*    Winterberry    **D** 8'

A deciduous shrub, native to northern and central U. S. in swamp areas, grown in moist acid soil, female plants with abundant fruit in winter, cut for decorations, *I. laevigata* is similar.

*Juniperus*    Juniper    **C**

An important genus of evergreens varying from tall trees to ground cover, tolerates hot, sunny dry conditions, suitable for most parts of the U. S., several cultivars are named.

*J. chinensis*    Chinese Juniper    **C**

Cv. 'Glauca Hetzi', dense to 15', light bluish foliage; cv. 'Ketelieri', broadly pyramidal, one of the best; cv. 'Pfitzeriana' popular shrubby type,; cv. 'Pfitzeriana Aurea' with young foliage yellow green.

*J. communis*    Common Juniper    **C**

Cv. 'communis depressa' - Prostrate Juniper, 2 to 3' and spreading branches, turns brownish in cold winter; cv. 'Stricta' - Irish Juniper, dark green foliage, narrow, columnar.

*J. conferta*    Shore Juniper    **C.**

A low spreading plant to 1' tall, suitable for ocean seashore areas.

*J. horizontalis*    Creeping Juniper    **C**

Cv. 'Bar Harbor', prostrate, more compact growing than the species; cv. 'Dougalassi' - Waukegan Juniper, steel blue foliage turning purplish in the fall; cv. 'Plumosa' - Andorra Juniper slow compact growth, gray green; cv. 'Blue Rug'-blue green foliage, grows close to the ground.

*J. virginiaka*   Eastern Red Cedar   **C**
Cultivars should be selected for uniformity; cv. 'Canaertii' compact pyramidal habit of growth; cv. 'Elegantissima' - Goldtip Red Cedar, young tips of branches golden tipped; cv. 'Globosa' - rounded, densely branched plant.

*Kalmia latifolia*   Mt. Laurel   **BLE** 10'
Requires acid soil and conditions similar to Rhododendron, native to eastern United States, flowers white, light pink to red, selected forms are occasionally sold with darker colored flowers.

*Kerria japonica*   Kerria   **D** 5'
Flowers yellow, single or double, in May, stems green, double flowered form is Pleniflora, most widely grown, tops may winterkill to soil line in severe winters, prune out oldest shoots after flowering.

*Kolkwitzia amabilis*   Beautybush   **D** 10'
Bellshaped pink flowers in May - June, dense habit of growth, prune out old shoots after flowering.

*Lagerstroemia indica*   Crape Myrtle   **D** 20'
A shrub or small tree flowering in mid summer with showy pink, red, purple or white flowers, prune in early spring, interesting exfoliating bark on old stems, foliage red in fall.

*Lavandula officinalis*   Lavender   **BLE** 2'
Aromatic gray foliage evergreen with spikes of blue flowers in June-July, grow in full sun, loose well drained soil, dried flower spikes used for fragrance.

*Ligustrum*   Privet
Both deciduous and evergreen species in this popular genus, useful for hedges or group plantings, several with white or yellow variegated leaf forms.

*L. amurense*   Amur Privet   **D** 10'
Resembles California Privet but leaves not as glossy, hardiest of the species.

*L. japonicum*   Japanese Privet   **BLE** 15'
Glossy dark green leaves, flowers white in clusters in summer also a variegated form but less vigorous.

*L. lucidum*   Glossy Privet   **BLE** to 30'
Potentially a small tree in the south, leaves 3 to 5'' long, often mixed in the trade with the Japanese privet.

*L. obtusifolium regalianium*   Regal Privet   **D** 5'
A horizontal branched form of the species, attractive as a specimen or used as an unclipped hedge.

*L. ovalifolium*   California Privet   **D** 15'
Widely used as a sheared hedge, winterkills at temperatures below

10°F, deciduous in the north in the fall, in milder climates hold leaves to spring.

*Magnolia*

A genus of small to large flowering trees. Those listed are suitable for smaller landscapes because of their ultimate size.

*M. grandiflora*    Southern or Bull Magnolia    **BLE** 40'

The classic tree of the South, large white flowers in summer, fragrant, hardy in areas with temperature not lower than 10°F.

*M. soulangeana*    Saucer Magnolia    **D** 15'

A hybrid of *M. denudata* and *M. liliflora* with many forms, a large shrub or small tree with several stems, flowers in early spring, flower color varies from white to pink to purplish, many with color on outside of petal and white inside popular cultivars include, 'Alba' - white with outside of petals light purple; cv. 'Alexandrina' - rose purple on outside and white inside; cv. 'Lennei' - purple outside, white inside; cv. 'Rustica' - rose red.

*M. stellata*    Star Magnolia    **D** 15'

Flowers white to pink, early spring, small shrubby habit of growth.

*M. virginiana*    Sweet Bay Magnolia    **BLE** 25'

Potentially a large tree but slow growing, tolerates moist soil, deciduous in northern limits, will stand temperatures to about zero, fragrant white flowers in late June - July.

*Mahonia aquafolium*    Oregon Holly Grape    **BLE** 3'

Dark green foliage that becomes bronze in winter, prune in spring to keep compact, yellow flowers in May followed with blue black fruit.

*M. bealii*    Leatherleaf Mahonia    **BLE** 10'

Long compound leaves with 9 to 15 leaflets, yellow flower clusters early in the spring with bluish black grapelike fruits, best grown in partial shade, foliage becomes bronze in fall, especially when in full sun.

*Nandina domestica*    Nandina    **BLE** 8'

Leaves twice or thrice compound turning red bronze in fall, flowers white in clusters in July with bright red berries in fall and winter, grow in full sun for most dense growth.

*Osmanthus heterophyllus*    Holly Osmanthus    **BLE** 15'

An opposite leaved plant with leaves resembling the American Holly, also listed as *O. ilicifolius,* hardy to about 10°F, white flowers in fall, fragrant, dense growth, suitable as a hedge where hardy.

*Paeonia suffruiticosa*    Tree Peony    **D** 5'

A woody species, plant in well drained soil, must not lack for water in summer, flowers large, usually double, similar to the herbaceous peony, white, pink, red, salmon and yellow, in May - June, many cultivars, propagated by grafting.

*Philadelphus*    Mockorange    **D**

A genus of early summer flowering shrubs, variable in size and with many cultivars, single or double white flowered shrubs with fragrance, plant in full sun.

*Picea glauca conica*    Dwarf White Spruce    **C** 20'

Spruce are generally not well adapted to city conditions, this dwarf white spruce is a slow growing pyramidal shaped plant, there are dwarf forms of other species as well.

*Pieris*

One of the most valuable of broad leaf evergreens for gardens, belongs to same group of plants as Rhododendron and have same cultural requirements, all flower in early spring with terminal clusters of white flowers, buds prominent in winter.

*P. floribunda*    Mountain Andromeda    **BLE** 5'

Native of eastern U. S. Va. to Ga., plants multibranched, with flowered clusters in a vertical position.

*P. forrestii*    Chinese Pieris    **BLE** 6'

A species best adapted to areas where temperatures do not go below 10°F, least hardy of cultivated species, new growth in spring scarlet red later turning green.

*P. japonica*    Japanese Pieris    **BLE** 8'

The most widely grown species with many cultivars including those with variegated foliage, flower clusters drooping.

*P. taiwanensis*    Formosa Pieris    **BLE** 6'

A broad leafed species with cluster of long racemes of white flowers, resembles the Japanese Pieris.

*Pinus*    Pine    **C**

Pines are decorative evergreens but generally to large for small gardens, several dwarf forms are somewhat shrub like, the following is the most widely used of the dwarf types.

*P. mugo mugo*    Mugho Pine    **C** 5'

Dwarf, slow growth usually with several upright stems, compact.

*Pittosporum tobira*    Japanese Pittosporum    **BLE** 10'

An attractive leathery leaf evergreen suitable for mild areas of the southern and Pacific states, flowers a creamy white in clusters in May, also a variegated form, suitable as a cool greenhouse plant.

*Poncirus trifoliata*    Hardy Orange    **BLE** 30'

A relative of the orange that tolerates temperatures to 15°F, evergreen but drops its leaves in cold winters, white flowers in late April with small orange fruits in fall, about 2½'' in diameter, filled with seed and very acid juice, the long thorns makes it useful for hedges.

*Potentilla fruiticosa*    Shrub Cinquefoil    **D** 3'

Small shrubby plants with white or yellowish flowers in July to frost, dense in habit of growth, grow in full sun, tolerates poor dry soil but prefers better growing conditions.

*Prunus*

Best known as the flowering cherries, peaches or plums, many may be too large for a small garden, the following shrubs are satisfactory garden kinds.

*P. laurocerasus*    Cherry Laurel    **BLE** 10'

A shrub with heavy leathery leaves, glossy green, racemes of white flowers in June, hardy to 15°F, useful as hedges in more southern locations, may show winter injury northern areas, cv. 'Schipkaensis' is most winter hardy form.

*P. triloba*    Flowering Almond    **D** 10'

Most effective because of display of double pink flowers in late spring before the leaves appear, not a showy plant otherwise.

*Pyracantha coccinea*    Scarlet Firethorn    **BLE** 10'

Widely grown for its orange or red fruits in the fall that are effective for several months, flowers white, in clusters in May - June, leaves deciduous in the north, several cultivars: cv. 'Aurea' - with yellow fruit; cv. 'Lelandii' red fruit and one of the hardiest; cv. 'Thornless' and cv. 'Sensation' with orange fruit.

*Rhododendron*

A large genus of evergreen and deciduous species for gardens, includes those plants called Azaleas, certain species tolerate temperatures below zero while others injured at 20°F., many hybrids within species and between species, requires an acid soil, moist but well drained.

*R. calendulaceum*    Flame Azalea    **D** 10'

A native with yellow, orange or reddish orange flowers in June, effective because of color range.

*R. catawbiense*    Catawba Rhododendron    **BLE** 10'

A native of the Appalachian Mountains from Va. south, a parent of the large flowering May - June flowering cultivars, flowers white, pink, red, violet and purple.

*R. indicum*    Indian Azalea    **BLE** 10'

One parent of the many garden azaleas of the southeastern United States and those used for greenhouse culture, large showy flowers, most do not stand temperatures below 20°F.

*R. mollis*    Mollia Azalea    **D** 10'

A species with golden yellow flowers and a parent in the development of Knaphill, Exbury and Mollis hybrids, temperatures to 10°F, flowers white, yellow, orange, apricot and reddish orange.

*R. mucronulatum*    Korean Rhododendron    **D** 6'
Very early flowering species with lavender pink flowers, useful as a companion plant with Forsythia, foliage yellow in fall.

*R. obtusum*    Kurume Azalea    **BLE** 8'
A parent in the development of the Kurume azaleas, Gable hybrids and others, many of these tolerate cold to 10°F or less, flower buds more temperature sensitive than vegetative tissue, important for garden use and as a greenhouse plant.

*Rosa*    Roses    **D**
The flowering roses, - the hybrid tea, hybrid perpetual, floribunda, and climbing roses are well adapted to small gardens; the miniature roses growing only 8 to 15'' tall are useful as edging plants and the shrub roses may be used with other shrubs in a border planting.

*Rosmarinus officinalis*    Rosemary    **BLE** 4'
This aromatic shrub is used in California and areas where winter temperature is mild, grown for its gray green foliage and blue flowers as well as its herb value, prune in early spring.

*Ruscus aculeatus*    Butchers Broom    **BLE** 2'
A low growing evergreen, stiff foliage, forms a compact plant, pest free, increase slowly.

*Santolina chamaecyparissus*    Lavender Cotton    **BLE** 1½'
Shrubby evergreen with silver gray wooly leaves with yellow daisy flowers in mid summer, grown as an edging or foreground plant, prune in early spring to shape plant, will stand shearing as a small hedge.

*Sarcococca hookeriana humilis*    Himalayan Sarcococca    **BLE** 2'
This is the dwarf form of the species with dark green leathery leaves, used as a ground cover or companion plant with other evergreen plants.

*Skimmia japonica*    Japanese Skimmia    **BLE** 2'
Bright glossy evergreen foliage with white flowers in spring and red fruits in the fall that remain on the plant for months, male and female flowers on separate plants, best foliage color in partial shade.

*Spiraea billiardii*    Billiard Spirea    **D** 5'
A useful plant in poor soil, dry areas, spreads by underground stems and forms a dense mat, rose-colored flowers in upright panicles in mid summer.

*S. bumalda*    'Anthony Waterer'    **D** 2'
A dwarf multistem plant, widely planted for its rose-pink flowers in clusters in mid summer to frost.

*S. vanhouttei*    Vanhoutte Spirea    **D** 5'
A familiar white flowering shrub with graceful arching branches, prune out oldest stems after flowering.

*Syringa vulgaris*    Common Lilac    **D** 8 to 10'

The well known lilac is a favorite of northern gardens with fragrant white, pink, lavender or purple flowers in May - June, in large panicles, single or double, many cultivars.

*S. persica*    Persian Lilac    **D** 8'

Smaller panicles of flowers than the common lilac, but flowers just ahead of it, color lavender to rosy pink, multistemmed plant, prolific in bloom.

*Tamarix pentandra*    Tamarisk    **D** 10 to 12'

A hardy plant with small feathery flowers, pink, borne on current seasons growth, hardiest of the species, tolerates seaside gardens.

*Taxus baccata*    English Yew    **C** 40'

The cultivar 'Repandens' is a hardy low growing form of this plant, hardy to about 10°F., useful for sun or shade.

*T. cuspidata nana*    Dwarf Japanese Yew    **C** 6 to 8'

A slow growing compact cultivar of the Japanese yew, plant in soils slightly acid to neutral.

*Thuja occidentalis*    American Arborvitae    **C**

Many forms of this species are grown, usually selected on the basis of good lasting color of the foliage and habit of growth as pyramidal, columnar or globe shaped.

*T. orientalis*    Oriental Arborvitae    **C**

Many forms of this species are grown although not as winter hardy as the American Arborvitae in the north, the better cultivars include 'Aurea', low growing with yellow foliage, compact; cv. 'Berckmann' golden yellow foliage which becomes more green by fall; cv. 'Globosa' with a globe habit of growth.

*Viburnum*

A genus of many species and cultivars of deciduous and evergreen kinds with generally showy flowers and fleshy berry-like fruits. Most grow best in full sun.

*V. burkwoodi*    Burkwood Viburnum    **BLE** 6'

A hybrid of *V. carlesii* and *V. utile* with fragrant light pink flowers, deciduous in colder climates, preferred to *V. carlesii*.

*V. carlcephalum*    Fragrant Snowball    **BLE** 8'

Another hybrid with a rounded flower cluster, up to 5'' in diameter, fragrant.

*V. carlesii*    Fragrant Viburnum    **BLE** 5'

The most fragrant of the viburnums, white clusters in early spring, susceptible to gray blight disease and the two previously mentioned species are preferred.

*V. dentatum*     Arrowwood    **D** 10'

A native species with many stems from base of plant, very cold hardy, use in sun or partial shade, rapid growing, bluish fruit in fall with reddish foliage.

*V. opulus*     European Cranberry bush     **D** 10'

A large, wide spreading plant with white flowers, red fruit in fall, cv. Compactum is more dense and compact; cv. 'Nanum', is 2 to 3' tall, dense, compact and generally doesnot flower; cv. 'Sterile' is the common Snowball but less satisfactory as it is very susceptible to aphid injury.

*V. plicatum*     Japanese Snowball    **D** 8 to 10'

Also sold as *V. tomentosum plicatum,* horizontal branching habit, with flower clusters borne on the upper side of the stem, cv. 'Mariesii', fruits red and produced in abundance; cv. 'Roseum', produces sterile pink flowers.

*V. rhytophyllum*     Leatherleaf Viburnum     **BLE** 15'

Large leathery leaves, crinkled, grayish or yellowish green with felty hairs, flower clusters white, not especially showy, hardy to about 10°F.

*Vinca minor*     Periwinkle myrtle     **BLE** 1'

A ground cover plant, non-woody but widely grown in sun and shade, foliage dark green, blue flowers in April - May, increases rapidly in well drained fertile soil, forms with variegated foliage generally less vigorous.

*Weigela florida*     Weigela    **D** 8'

A reliable flowering shrub with generally pink to white flowers in May - June, pest free, prune out oldest stems after flowering, select named cultivars for best flowers, cv. 'Candida' - white flowers that do not fade to pink; cv. 'Bristol Ruby' - red flowers; cv. 'Vanicekii', one of the hardiest and best of red flowering kinds; cv. 'Variegata' - pink to white flowers, variegated green and white foliage.

*Yucca filamentosa*     Adams Needle     **BLE** 3'

A non-woody plant with long sword like leaves terminating in a sharp point, large panicle of white flowers in mid summer, this species hardy throughout the U. S., excellent companion plant with other evergreens because of foliage contrast, other species suitable in southern locations.